INTIMATE
VIOLENCE
IN
FAMILIES

FAMILY STUDIES TEXT SERIES

Series Editor: RICHARD J. GELLES, *University of Rhode Island*
Series Associate Editor: ALEXA A. ALBERT, *University of Rhode Island*

This series of textbooks is designed to examine topics relevant to a broad view of family studies. The series is aimed primarily at undergraduate students of family sociology and family relations, among others. Individual volumes will be useful to students in psychology, home economics, counseling, human services, social work, and other related fields. Core texts in the series cover such subjects as theory and conceptual design, research methods, family history, cross-cultural perspectives, and life course analysis. Other texts will cover traditional topics, such as dating and mate selection, parenthood, divorce and remarriage, and family power. Topics that have been receiving more recent public attention will also be dealt with, including family violence, later life families, and fatherhood.

Because of their wide range and coverage, Family Studies Texts can be used singly or collectively to supplement a standard text or to replace one. These books will be of interest to both students and professionals in a variety of disciplines.

Volumes in this series:

1. LATER LIFE FAMILIES, Timothy H. Brubaker
2. INTIMATE VIOLENCE IN FAMILIES, Second Edition
   Richard J. Gelles & Claire Pedrick Cornell
3. BECOMING A PARENT, Ralph LaRossa
4. FAMILY RESEARCH METHODS, Brent C. Miller
5. PATHS TO MARRIAGE, Bernard I. Murstein
6. WORK AND FAMILY LIFE, Patricia Voydanoff
7. REMARRIAGE, Marilyn Ihinger-Tallman & Kay Pasley
8. FAMILY STRESS MANAGEMENT, Pauline Boss
9. DIVORCE, Sharon J. Price & Patrick C. McKenry
10. FAMILIES AND HEALTH,
    William J. Doherty & Thomas L. Campbell
11. VARIANT LIFESTYLES AND RELATIONSHIPS,
    Bram P. Buunk & Barry van Driel
12. ADOLESCENT SEXUALITY AND PREGNANCY,
    Patricia Voydanoff & Brenda W. Donnelly

Richard J. Gelles
and
Claire Pedrick Cornell

INTIMATE
VIOLENCE
IN
FAMILIES
Second Edition

FAMILY STUDIES
TEXT SERIES **2**

SAGE PUBLICATIONS
The International Professional Publishers
Newbury Park   London   New Delhi

For information address:

SAGE Publications, Inc.
2455 Teller Road
Newbury Park, California 91320

SAGE Publications Ltd.
6 Bonhill Street
London EC2A 4PU
United Kingdom

SAGE Publications India Pvt. Ltd.
M-32 Market
Greater Kailash I
New Delhi 110 048 India

Printed in the United States of America

Library of Congress Cataloging-in-Publication Data

Gelles, Richard J.
        Intimate violence in families / Richard J. Gelles and Claire
Pedrick Cornell. -- 2nd ed.
            p.   cm. -- (Family studies text series ; v. 2)
        Includes bibliographical references.
        ISBN 0-8039-3718-0. -- ISBN 0-8039-3719-9 (pbk.)
        1. Family violence--United States.   I. Cornell, Claire Pedrick.
II. Title.   III. Series.
HQ809.3.U5G443   1990
362.82'92--dc20   90-31861
                                                                                     CIP

        95   96   97   98   99   16   15   14   13   12   11

To the memory of
Barry A. Marks

Contents

Acknowledgments   9

1. Introduction   11

    Myths That Hinder Understanding of
      Family Violence   12
    What Is Violent and Abusive?   20
    Discussion Questions   24
    Suggested Assignments   24

2. Violence Between Intimates: Historical Legacy—
   Contemporary Approval   25

    The Historical Legacy of Family Violence   26
    Family Violence Around the World   28
    The Social Transformation of Family Violence   31
    Contemporary Attitudes   38
    Summing Up   40
    Discussion Questions   41
    Suggested Assignments   41

3. The Youngest Victims: Violence Toward Children   42

    The Extent of Violence and Maltreatment   43
    Who Are the Abusers/Who Is Abused?   53
    Consequences of Child Abuse   61
    Discussion Questions   63
    Suggested Assignments   63

4. The "Appropriate" Victims: Women   64

    Courtship Violence   65
    Extent of Marital Violence   66
    Factors Associated with Wife Abuse   72
    Staying in or Leaving Battering
      Relationships   78
    A Note on Husbands as Victims   81
    Discussion Questions   82
    Suggested Assignments   83

5. **Hidden Victims: Siblings, Adolescents, Parents, and the Elderly**   84

   Sibling Violence   85
   Violence Toward Adolescents   90
   Parent Abuse   95
   Elder Abuse   100
   Summary   104
   Discussion Questions   105
   Suggested Assignments   105

6. **Explaining Family Violence**   106

   Profiles of Violent Homes   106
   Violence and the Organization of Family Life   108
   Models That Explain Family Violence   111
   An Exchange/Social Control Theory of Family Violence   115
   Toward Preventing and Treating Family Violence   121
   Discussion Questions   121
   Suggested Assignments   121

7. **Prevention and Treatment: Society's Response and Responsibility**   122

   From Behind Closed Doors: Recognizing Family Violence   123
   Intervention in Family Violence: Compassion or Control   126
   Treatment   128
   Prevention   138
   Discussion Questions   140
   Suggested Assignment   140

References   141
Author Index   152
Subject Index   155
About the Authors   159

Acknowledgments

THIS BOOK OWES MUCH to our previous work and writings on family violence. A number of our colleagues and friends have been particularly helpful over the years and have assisted in considering the difficult and complex issues that surround family violence. Murray Straus has been a teacher, colleague, and sounding board for the past 20 years. Eli and Carolyn Newberger and the entire Family Development Study at Children's Hospital Medical Center, Boston, have also been colleagues and friends for the same two decades. They opened up the world of clinical practice to us, and their help and support have been invaluable. Bud Bolton also helped guide us through the trials and tribulations of applying research to practice and policy. Our students at the University of Rhode Island, especially the students in Sociology 420: Family Violence, have provided us insight and useful ideas for a text on family violence. Joanne Lawrence provided invaluable typing and clerical help in preparing this second edition.

Finally, our respective spouses, Winton Cornell and Judy Gelles, provided critical, social, and emotional support. Jason Gelles (age 15) and David Gelles (age 12) continue to be sources of inspiration. Since the first edition both have developed into writers, playwrights, and songwriters.

Funding for the research reported in this book came from NIMH Grants MH 27557 and MH 40027.

CHAPTER
1

Introduction

PEOPLE ARE MORE LIKELY to be killed, physically assaulted, hit, beaten up, slapped, or spanked in their own homes by other family members than anywhere else, or by anyone else, in our society. Some observers (Straus, Gelles, & Steinmetz, 1976) have proposed that violence in the family is more common than love.

Not only are these facts true today, they are true throughout the history of the United States. Not only do these statements apply to American families, they are also accurate assessments of family life in England, western Europe, and many other countries and societies around the globe.

We do not commonly think of the family as society's most violent social institution. Typically, family life is thought to be warm, intimate, stress reducing, and the place that people *flee to* for safety. Our desire to idealize family life is partly responsible for a tendency either not to see family violence or to condone it as being a necessary and important part of raising children, relating to spouses, and conducting other family transactions.

This text is designed to provide a basic overview of the subject of family violence. Many books take a look at only one aspect of violence and maltreatment in the home. Typically, a writer will discuss child abuse, wife abuse, or elder abuse, but very rarely do books and articles attempt to examine all aspects of violence in families and try to look at the whole picture of family violence. While it is important to understand the nature and causes of child abuse or wife abuse, concentrating on just one form of violence or abuse may obscure the entire picture and hinder a complete understanding of the causes and consequences of abuse. A case example of the problems produced by narrowly focusing on just one type of abuse is illustrated by the experience of a hospital-based child abuse diagnostic team. The team was discussing the case of a 6-month-old child who had received a fractured skull. After reviewing the medical reports and results of interviews with both parents, it was concluded that a 5-year-old sibling had caused the damage by striking the infant. All in the room breathed a sigh of relief. Now, they concluded, they would not have to file a child abuse report. Just as they were about to break up, satisfied with the consensus they had arrived at, a physician commented, "But how do you suppose the 5-year-old learned to be violent?" Back they went to the table for a two-hour discussion about whether or not the violence of a 5-year-old was cause for a child abuse report.

This case dramatically illustrates that one form of family violence may be closely connected to other acts of violence in the home. To focus on just one type of family violence often causes one to miss the overall picture. As important, especially for this text, is that one can only understand, explain, treat, and prevent family violence by understanding the operation and function of the entire family system.

MYTHS THAT HINDER
UNDERSTANDING OF FAMILY VIOLENCE

How is it possible that families have been violent for centuries, all over the globe, and we have only recently discovered and attended to family violence as a serious family and social problem? How is it that, after 20 years of intensive research and practice in this field, we can still read newspaper accounts that talk about instances where children who were identified by social service agencies as abused, and whose cases had been followed by social workers for months, are killed, virtually under the nose of the person who was supposed to protect them? One answer for these two questions is that there are a number of myths about family violence that tend to hinder both public recognition of the problem and effective professional practice. This text is designed to explode many of the conventional myths about family violence and replace these myths with knowledge derived from scholarly research on family violence. As a preview of the issues that will be taken up in the text, and as a means of clearing the decks of some of the more popular and persistent myths, this section presents and then debunks the major myths hindering our understanding of family violence.

Myth 1: Family Violence Is Rare

Until the 1960s, most people considered family violence a rare phenomenon. What few official statistics there were tended to bear out this assumption. Few states required professionals or members of the public to report known or suspected instances of child abuse. When David Gil (1970) surveyed the entire country in 1967 to determine how many valid cases of child abuse there were, he found that there were about 6,000. The numbers of abused children varied state by state, speaking more about the procedures used to locate abused children than the actual occurrence of abuse. California had more than 3,500 reports, and Rhode Island none. Until recently there were few localities or states that recorded cases of spouse abuse. Today, only three states collect official data on the abuse of adults. Prior to 1970, few hospitals bothered to categorize women patients they treated as either abused or nonabused. Police departments did keep records of how many domestic disturbance calls they received and investigated, but many times the records were inaccurate or incomplete. Sometimes a husband assaulting his wife would be recorded as a domestic disturbance; other times it would be recorded as an assault.

The strong belief that families are places people turn *to* for help, and the perception that city streets hold the greatest risk for women and children, help to continue the myth of the rareness of family violence even into the 1990s. As different types of family violence are discovered and examined, most people find it difficult to believe how many individuals and families are involved in violence in the home.

Myth 2: Family Violence Is Confined to Mentally Disturbed or Sick People

A woman drowns her twin 6-month-old daughters. Another mother throws her daughter off a bridge into icy water. A mother and father plunge their 4-year-old into a bathtub filled with boiling water. A father has sexual intercourse with his 6-month-old daughter. A woman waits for her husband to take a shower, then fires a bullet into his skull at close range with a .357 magnum.

These descriptions, and accompanying color slides of the harm done to the victims, are usually enough to convince most people that only someone who is mentally disturbed or truly psychotic would inflict such grievous harm onto a defenseless child, woman, or man. One way of upholding the image of the nurturant and safe family is to combine the myth that family violence is rare with the myth that only "sick" people abuse family members. Combining the two myths allows us to believe that, when and if violence does take place, it is the problem of "people other than us." An example of this is the manner in which family violence is portrayed in literature, television, or the movies. The sociologists Murray Straus and Suzanne Steinmetz (Steinmetz & Straus, 1974) reviewed American fiction, television shows, and movies for examples of family violence. First, they found violence between family members infrequently portrayed. When there was an incident of violence, it almost always involved a violent act committed by someone who was a criminal (the violent son in the movie *The Godfather*), foreign (the comic strip *Andy Capp*), or drunk (Rhett Butler in *Gone with the Wind*). The message conveyed by the media is that normal people do not hit family members.

The manner by which people determine that abusers are sick undermines the claim of mental illness. "People who abuse women and children are sick," we are told. How do you know they are sick? "Because they abuse women and children." This explanation does nothing more than substitute the word *sick* for *abuse*. The key question is, without knowing what someone did to his or her spouse or child, could you accurately diagnose him or her as mentally ill? In most cases, this is impossible. The sociologist Murray Straus (1980) claims that fewer than 10% of all instances of family violence are caused by mental illness or psychiatric disorders.

Myth 3: Family Violence Is Confined to the Lower Class

The death of Lisa Steinberg in New York City in November 1987 captured national attention. The New York City police were called to a Greenwich Village apartment early one morning by a woman, Ms. Hedda Nussbaum, who said her daughter, Elizabeth, was choking on food. When they arrived, the police found 6-year-old Lisa Steinberg barely breathing. Her 18-month-old brother, Michael, was tied to his playpen with some twine and stood in urine soaked clothes. Elizabeth Steinberg died a week later. Joel Steinberg, an attorney, and Hedda Nussbaum, a former editor of children's books, were charged with the murder of Lisa. Joel Steinberg was later found guilty and sentenced to 25 years in jail.

Lisa Steinberg's death and the trial and conviction of Joel Steinberg set off a media blitz. Newspaper articles, television shows, and radio talk shows delved into the case for nearly two years. The case led to one novel and numerous other books and articles about domestic violence. Why would a single case capture so much attention? One plausible explanation is that the case of Lisa Steinberg, Joel Steinberg, and Hedda Nussbaum did not conform to the stereotype of child and wife abuse. Joel Steinberg was a 46-year-old criminal lawyer. Hedda Nussbaum, who had lived with Steinberg for 17 years, was a former editor of children's books for Random House. Their apartment was not a tenement in an urban ghetto but was in an upscale building where Mark Twain had once lived.

Next to the myth of mental illness, the next most pervasive myth about family violence is that it is confined to the lower class. Like all myths, there is a grain of truth behind this belief. Researchers do find more reported violence and abuse among the lower class. The psychologist George Levinger studied applicants for divorce and learned that 40% of the working-class applicants indicated that abuse was the reason they were seeking the divorce. Of the middle-class applicants, 23% also mentioned violence as the motivation for wanting to end the marriage (Levinger, 1966). Official reports of child abuse indicate an overwhelming overrepresentation of lower-class families being reported as abusers. However, by virtue of being in the lower class, families run a greater risk of being correctly *and falsely* labeled "abusers" if their children are seen with injuries (Newberger et al., 1977). Believing that abuse of wives and children is confined to the lower class is yet another way people try to see acts of others as deviant and their own behavior as normal.

Myth 4: Family Violence Occurs in All Groups— Social Factors Are Not Relevant

When the first medical practitioners began to notice and attend to cases of child abuse, one of the first things they were struck by was that the children came from every type of social, racial, economic, and age group. This finding shattered the myth of violence being confined to the lower class, but that myth was replaced by the belief that social factors were not related to child abuse and family violence. If the children of lawyers, doctors, and corporate executives are being abused along with children of unemployed truck drivers, how then can social class or poverty be a cause of child abuse?

There are two problems with this observation and the belief that social factors are not relevant in explaining family violence. First, for a factor to be a cause of child abuse, it does not have to be perfectly associated with abuse. For poverty to be a causal factor, it is not necessary that only poor people abuse children and no well-to-do people are abusive. There are very few (perhaps no) perfect associations in social science. Thus, for social factors to be causal, they need only satisfy the four criteria of causality: (a) association (statistical, not deterministic); (b) time order (the cause must precede the consequences); (c) nonspuriousness (no third factor, preceding cause and effect in time, is related to both cause and effect); and (d) rationale (the proposed relationship has to make logical sense). The second problem with the observation that social factors are not related is that they are. Even though abuse can be found among the wealthy and the poor, it is more likely to be found among the poor. Even though most poor people do not abuse their children, there is indeed a greater risk of abuse among those in the lowest income groups. We will examine the relationship between social factors and family violence in Chapters 3 and 4.

Myth 5: Children Who Are Abused Will Grow Up to Be Child Abusers

This is a myth with some truth value to it. Virtually all studies of child abuse find that abusive adults were more likely to have been treated harshly and abused as children than adults who are not abusive. The problem with the statement that "children who are abused will grow up to be child abusers" is that this is a deterministic statement and the relationship is probabilistic. People who experience abuse are *more likely*, but not preprogrammed, to become violent adults. Sadly, many people have begun to believe that *all* abused children grow up to be violent. This belief has two sad and negative consequences. First, it scares people who have experienced violence as children into thinking that they are "preprogrammed" to be violent and that perhaps they should avoid marriage and having children. Second, those who are responsible for detecting and treating child abuse may see an unusual injury in a child and, upon learning that a parent had been battered as a child, assume that the parent has caused the injury. False positive diagnoses (labeling someone an abuser when he or she is not) are a possible consequence of believing that violence determines violence.

Again, just as with social factors, it is important to remember that perfect associations rarely exist in social science. Abuse and violence grow out of a complex set of interrelated factors (as we will find in Chapters 3 through 5), and latching onto one commonsense factor misrepresents the causal explanation and can cause injustice.

Myth 6: Battered Wives Like Being Hit, Otherwise They Would Leave

One of the controversies that surrounded the case of Lisa Steinberg was why Hedda Nussbaum had endured years of physical abuse and why she was unable to protect Lisa from the violence and brutality of Joel Steinberg. More than one observer, including the feminist author Susan Brownmiller, condemned Nussbaum for her inability to protect herself and Lisa.

One common question asked about battered women is this: "Why don't they (the battered wives) just pack up and leave?" Battered women fail to attract the same attention and sympathy directed toward battered children because, somehow, many people think that the women (a) provoked the violence and (b) must like it if they didn't leave after the first beating. Those who espouse this view (and it is a belief of both men and women) tend to be those with considerable education, good jobs, and extensive social networks. They cannot imagine that someone could be socially, legally, and materially entrapped in a marriage. They cannot imagine that a woman could literally have no place to go. Wives seem to bear the brunt of considerable "victim blaming." Quite a few people believe that battered wives are somehow culpable, and their culpability is enforced by their decision not to leave. Nothing could be further from the truth. This issue will be discussed at length in Chapter 4.

Myth 7: Alcohol and Drug Abuse Are the
Real Causes of Violence in the Home

The "demon rum" explanation for abuse in the home is nearly as popular as the mental illness explanation, and perhaps more popular than the two social class myths. Again, certain facts help support the myth. Most studies find a considerable association between drinking and violence (Gelles, 1974; Gillen, 1946; Guttmacher, 1960; Snell, Rosenwald, & Robey, 1964; Wolfgang, 1958). In cases of spousal violence, both offender *and* victim have frequently been drinking before the violence. Perhaps as many as half the instances of violence and abuse involve some alcohol or drugs—a very strong association. But, do the drugs or the alcohol themselves cause people to be violent? Are drugs and alcohol disinhibitors that unleash violent behavior? And, would solving the drug or drinking problem eliminate the violence? Common sense frequently says "yes" to these questions. Research argues "no." There is little evidence that alcohol and drugs are disinhibitors. The best evidence against the disinhibitor theory comes from cross-cultural studies of drinking behavior. These studies find that how people react to drinking varies from culture to culture (MacAndrew & Edgerton, 1969). In some cultures people drink and become violent; in others, people drink and are passive. What explains the difference? The difference is due to what people in those societies believe about alcohol. If they believe it is a disinhibitor, people become disinhibited. If they believe that it is a depressant, people become depressed. Because our society believes that alcohol and drugs release violent tendencies, people are given a "time-out" from the normal rules of social behavior when they drink or when people believe they are drunk. Combine the time-out with the desire to "hush up" instances of family violence, and you have the perfect excuse: "I didn't know what I was doing, I was drunk." Or, from the victim's perspective, "My husband is a Dr. Jekyll and Mr. Hyde—when he drinks he is violent, when he is sober there is no problem." In the end, violent spouses and parents learn that, if they want not to be held responsible for their violence, they should either drink before they hit or at least say they were drunk.

Additional evidence comes from research on the link between alcohol and intimate violence. Murray Straus and his colleagues examined data from two national surveys of family violence. The first survey found that there was a strong relationship between alcohol abuse and family violence. However, extreme levels of alcohol abuse were not related to high levels of violence. Physical violence in families actually declined when drunkenness occurred "almost always" (Coleman & Straus, 1983). Kantor and Straus (1987) examined data from a second survey of family violence and again found that excessive drinking is associated with higher levels of wife abuse. However, in the majority of families, alcohol is not an immediate antecedent of violence.

More recently, drug abuse, especially "crack abuse," has been linked to extreme and severe cases of domestic violence. The issue of the possible link between drug abuse and violence is explosive, and fact is often mixed with myth. One problem is that there are multiple drugs that have been implicated in acts of violence, and each drug has a different physiological effect. In addition, there are varying social expectations for how specific drugs affect human behavior. Research on different forms of drugs and their possible impact on violence behavior have found some consistent evidence. Marijuana produces a euphoric effect and may reduce rather than increase the probability of violent behavior. Research on LSD also finds that the physiological effects of the drug are antithetical with violence. One type of drug does stand out as a possible cause of violent behavior—amphetamines. Amphetamines raise excitability and muscle tension. This may lead to impulsive behavior. The behavior that follows from amphetamine use is related to both the dosage and the preuse personality of the user. High-dosage users who already have aggressive personalities are likely to become more aggressive when using this drug (Johnson, 1972). Studies of nonhuman primates—stump tail macaques—have found that the monkeys do become more aggressive when they receive a protocol of *d*-amphetamine (Smith & Byrd, 1987). Based on his program of research with monkeys and amphetamines, Neil Smith estimates that as much as 5% of instances of physical child abuse are related to amphetamine use (Smith & Byrd, 1987).

Except for the evidence that appears to link amphetamine use to violence, the picture of the alcohol- and drug-crazed partner or parent who impulsively and violently abuses a family member is a distortion. If alcohol and other drugs are linked to violence at all, it is through a complicated set of individual, situational, and social factors.

Myth 8: Violence and Love Do Not Coexist in Families

Once people believe that families are violent, they tend to think that the violence occurs all the time. Moreover, the persistent belief is that, if family members are violent, they must not love one another. Violence, while common in many families, is certainly not the most frequent behavior in the home. As we will see in Chapters 3, 4, and 5, although violence and abuse are typically chronic problems in families and not simply one-shot events, on average, abusive parents and partners are violent about once every other month. The remaining time the family functions nonviolently (although the threat of physical violence and abuse tends to hang heavy in the air). It is not only possible, but probable, that abused wives still have strong feelings for their husbands. Many battered children love their parents in spite of the beatings. In fact, most victims of family violence are taught that they deserve the beatings, and thus they have the problem, not the attacker. That violence and love can coexist in a household is perhaps the most insidious aspect of family violence, because we grow up learning that it is acceptable to hit the people you love.

WHAT IS VIOLENT AND ABUSIVE?

One of the earliest and most enduring problems in the field of child abuse, wife abuse, and family violence has been to develop useful, clear, and acceptable definitions of *violence* and *abuse*. Those who have studied child abuse have tried for years to develop acceptable and accepted definitions and have found that after countless conferences, workshops, and publications there are perhaps as many definitions as there are scholars in the field.

An example of an early definition of child abuse was the one used by C. Henry Kempe and his colleagues (1962) in their article "The Battered Child Syndrome." Kempe, a physician, defined child abuse as a clinical condition (i.e., with diagnosable medical and physical symptoms) having to do with those who have been deliberately injured by a physical assault. This definition restricts abuse to only those acts of physical violence that produce a diagnosable injury. The National Center on Child Abuse and Neglect, an agency the federal government established in 1974, expanded the definition of abuse to include nonphysical acts as well. The agency's definition of abuse is the physical or mental injury, sexual abuse, negligent treatment, or maltreatment of a child under the age of eighteen by a person who is responsible for the child's welfare under circumstances which indicate that the child's health or welfare is harmed or threatened thereby. (Public Law [93-237])

This definition lumps acts of violence and nonviolence into the same definition. On one hand, definitions like those used by the National Center on Child Abuse and Neglect include acts that go well beyond physical violence. On the other hand, this definition is restrictive in that *only* acts of violence that cause an injury are considered abusive.

Force and Violence

If a father takes a gun and shoots at his child and misses, there is no physical injury and, according to many definitions of abuse, this act is not abuse. There is, of course, harm in a father shooting and missing, but the act itself does not qualify as abuse under the strict terms of the definitions. Ideally, then, a definition of abuse should include harmful acts that, for some reason (bad aim), do not produce an injury. At the other extreme, a father who spanks his child is not usually considered either abusive or violent. Most people believe that spanking a child is normal, necessary, and good. Nearly 90% of parents report that they spank their children, and some people believe that the true figure is a lot closer to 100%. As many as one in four men and one in six women think that under certain conditions it is appropriate for a husband to hit his wife (Stark & McEvoy, 1970). Consequently, some researchers believe that, in defining violence, it is a good idea to separate the so-called normal acts of "force" from the nonnormal and harmful acts of "violence." While such a separation might seem desirable, distinguishing between acceptable and unacceptable acts proves more difficult than one can imagine. One major question is this: Who decides which acts of violence are legitimate and illegitimate? Is "force" hitting a child without physical evidence of an injury, while "violence" is hitting a child and causing a black-and-blue mark? Should the decision be left to the person who is being hit, to the person doing the hitting, to agents of social control such as police, social workers, or judges? Should the decision be left to social scientists? An extensive study of the definitions of child abuse carried out by Jeanne Giovannoni and Rosina Becerra found that what is defined as "child abuse" varies by social category and profession. Police officers, social workers, physicians, and lawyers have differing views on what constitutes "child abuse." Similarly, the definition of abuse varies by social class, race, and ethnicity (Giovannoni & Becerra, 1979).

A Definition of Violence

In the end, the difficulty in defining what acts are violent and what acts are physical, but not violent, is due to varying cultural and subcultural views on whether certain behavior is or is not acceptable. It would be far too complex to have a definition that depended on the situation the behavior was used in, the size of the offender, the size of the victim, and the reactions of those who observed or heard about the behavior. For that reason, this text uses the definition of violence employed by a number of researchers. The definition views violence as "an act carried out with the intention or perceived intention of causing physical pain or injury to another person." The physical pain can range from slight pain, as in a slap, to murder. In order to deal with the commonsense assumption that spankings should be viewed differently from using weapons against wives or children, it is useful to consider two categories of the general definition of violence: "normal violence" and "abusive violence."

Normal violence. Normal violence consists of the commonplace slaps, pushes, shoves, and spankings that frequently are considered a normal or acceptable part of raising children or interacting with a spouse. These are the acts many people object to calling "violent." This is especially true of spanking. Family violence researchers who state their views on television or radio, or who are quoted in the press, constantly receive indignant letters from people who object to calling a spanking "violent." "Spare the rod and spoil the child." "I was spanked and I needed it." "My little one would be dead by now if I hadn't spanked him and let him know he shouldn't drink or eat certain things." These and other arguments, typically advanced by those who do the hitting, all focus on the physical acts that we consider "normal violence."

Abusive violence. The more dangerous acts of violence we shall refer to as "abusive violence." These acts are defined as acts that have the high potential for injuring the person being hit. Included in this definition are punches, kicks, bites, chokings, beatings, shootings, stabbings, or attempted shootings or stabbings.

The controversy in this definition is that it does not take into consideration what actually happened to the victims of the violence. By ignoring consequences, this definition is much broader than the more narrow definitions of child or wife abuse, which typically require that some diagnosable harm be inflicted. The reason for not being concerned about consequences is that research on assault and homicide, which has been carried out by criminologists, has consistently found that the things that differentiate injurious violence from violence that causes no harm are typically random phenomena such as aim or luck (Pittman & Handy, 1964; Pokorny, 1965; Wolfgang, 1958).

Why Just Physical Violence?

Hitting, punching, and shooting and other acts of physical violence do not exhaust the range of harmful acts committed by family members against other household members. Students of child maltreatment have identified neglect, emotional abuse, sexual abuse, educational neglect, medical neglect, and failure to thrive as forms of maltreatment. Feminists sometimes argue that pornography and some types of advertising are acts of violence against women (London, 1978). Why, then, confine this book to only physical violence? One reason is because it is important, theoretically and practically, to differentiate acts of physical violence from other harmful but nonviolent coercive acts (Etzioni, 1971). Physical violence is qualitatively different from other means of injuring people. Thus, although physical violence shares with other harm-producing acts the central characteristics of malevolence and harm-doing intent, the nature of the intended harm—physical pain and suffering—is unique. As the children's taunt goes: "Sticks and stones may break my bones, but names will never hurt me." Well, the names sometimes do hurt, but in a very different way. From a practical point of view, lumping all forms of malevolence and harm-doing together may muddy the water so much that it might be impossible to determine what causes abuse. While harmful acts may share some causes, other factors may be (and are) unique. Unless violence is treated separately from other acts, it may be difficult to determine both the causes and the solutions to family violence.

DISCUSSION QUESTIONS

(1) Why is it useful to examine all forms of family violence instead of concentrating on just one single type, such as child abuse?

(2) Why do the myths about family violence exist? What possible functions might the myths serve for people who treat family violence? For society?

(3) Discuss and critique the "alcohol as a disinhibitor" theory of the relationship between alcohol and family violence.

(4) Develop and critique your own definitions of *violence* and *abuse*.

SUGGESTED ASSIGNMENTS

(1) Locate newspaper articles that report family violence. What definitions of violence and abuse seem to be used in these articles? Are any of the myths included in the articles? Identify the common assumptions about the nature and causes of family violence in the articles.

(2) Locate articles on child abuse, sexual abuse, or spouse abuse in popular magazines (e.g., *Women's Day, Redbook, Family Circle, Time, Newsweek*). Compare how this issue is presented in popular magazines with the presentation found in newspapers. Locate one or more of the myths presented in this chapter in the magazine articles.

CHAPTER
2

Violence Between Intimates: Historical Legacy— Contemporary Approval

A DECADE AGO 10% of a national sample of Americans considered child abuse a serious problem. In 1982, nine out of ten people surveyed by Louis Harris and Associates thought that child abuse was a serious social problem. Has the problem increased ninefold, or have Americans just become more aware of the dimensions of the problem of violence in the family?

The belief that violence in the family is rare and the rapid increase in public awareness of intimate abuse have led many people to conclude that violence in the family is a new phenomenon that has increased in epidemic proportions in the last few years.

Violence between intimates is not new. Once, when we were asked about the problem of sibling violence, we were asked how far violence between siblings goes back in time. We responded, "Well, you can begin with Cain killing Abel in *Genesis.*" Similarly, there are other biblical descriptions of family violence. The first book of the Bible describes God's commandment that Abraham sacrifice his son Issac. Later, in the New Testament, Jesus was presumably saved from Herod's "slaughter of the innocents."

The question of whether we are more violent now than during previous times in history is difficult to answer. Selective inattention to the problem of intimate violence meant that official records of family violence have not been kept until the last two decades. Similarly, researchers have traditionally been reluctant to conduct surveys and ask questions about violence or abuse. Until recently (see Chapters 3 and 4), there had been no research conducted that attempted to measure the changing rates of violence toward children or between spouses.

The first section of this chapter reviews the historical legacy of family violence. Modern Americans neither are the first families to use violence on loved ones nor are we the only society in the world to be violent toward those we love. Next we explore the social transformation of violence. We trace the evolution of the issue of family violence from selective inattention, when nearly all that was written on violence in the home appeared on the front page of the *National Enquirer*, to the present, when violence between intimates is discussed and analyzed on television and radio talk shows, in television dramas, in national magazines, in legislative bodies, and by presidential task forces. The chapter concludes with a discussion of contemporary attitudes about intimate violence.

THE HISTORICAL LEGACY OF
FAMILY VIOLENCE

We take for granted that today's children have the right to live and grow to achieve their full developmental potential. The vocal and persistent debate on abortion centers on whether such rights should be extended to a newly conceived fetus in the womb. Women have fought for centuries for equal rights with men. We have begun to take for granted that women have a right to be treated the same as men. But what we now take for granted has not always been the case, and the history of the subordination of women and children is closely connected to the history and causes of violence and abuse in the family.

Infanticide and the Abuse of Children

The history of Western society is one in which children have been subjected to unspeakable cruelties. The historian Samuel Radbill (1980) reports that in ancient times infants had no rights until the right to live was ritually bestowed upon them by their fathers. When the right to live was withheld by fathers, infants were indeed abandoned or left to die. Although we do not know how often children were killed or abandoned, we do know that infanticide was widely accepted among ancient and prehistoric cultures. Infants could be put to death because they cried too much, because they were sickly or deformed, or because they had some perceived imperfection. Girls, twins, and the children of unmarried women were the special targets of infanticide (Robin, 1982).

Many societies also subjected their offspring to rituals or survival tests. Some North American Indians threw their newborns into pools of water and rescued them only if they rose to the surface and cried. The Greeks exposed their children to the natural elements as a survival test.

Infanticide was practiced through the Middle Ages. Lloyd DeMause (1974) has examined the history of childhood and graphically explains that by 1526 the latrines of Rome were said to "resound with the cries of children who had been plunged into them." Infanticide continued through the eighteenth and nineteenth centuries. Illegitimate children continue to run the greatest risk of infanticide even today. A few years ago an old steamer trunk was opened in a mill town in southern New Hampshire. Inside the trunk were a number of small skeletons, alleged to have been illegitimate children killed at birth.

Killing children was not the only form of abuse inflicted by generations of parents. From prehistoric times right through to colonial America, children have been mutilated, beaten, and maltreated. Such treatment was not only condoned, it was often mandated as the most appropriate child-rearing method. Children were hit with rods, canes, and switches. Boys have been castrated to produce eunuchs. Our forefathers in colonial America were implored to "beat the devil" out of their children. Stubborn child laws were passed that permitted parents to put to death unruly children, although it is not clear whether children were actually ever killed.

Women: The "Appropriate" Victims

The subordinate status of women in America and in most of the world's societies is well documented. Because physical force and violence is the ultimate resource that can be used to keep subordinate groups in their place, the history of women in European and American societies has been one in which women have been victims of physical assault.

The sociologists Rebecca and Russell Dobash (1979) claim that, in order to understand wife beating in contemporary society, one must understand and recognize the century-old legacy of women as the "appropriate" victims of family violence.

Roman husbands and fathers had control not only over their children but over their wives as well. A Roman husband could chastise, divorce, or kill his wife. Not only that, the behaviors for which these punishments were appropriate—adultery, public drunkenness, and attending public games—were the very same behaviors that Roman men engaged in daily (Dobash & Dobash, 1979)!

As with children, women are also victimized as far back as the Bible. Eve is blamed for eating the forbidden fruit. For Eve's transgression, the Bible tells us that all women are to be punished by having to bear children. The very same passage in *Genesis* that multiplies women's sorrow and calls for them to bear children also sanctions the husband's rule over his wife (Gen. 3:16).

Blackstone's codification of English common law in 1768 asserted that husbands had the right to "physically chastise" an errant wife provided that the stick was no thicker than his thumb—thus the "rule of thumb" was born. The legacy of British common law carried over into the United States well into the nineteenth century. In 1824 a Mississippi court set the precedent for allowing corporal punishment of wives by husbands. The precedent held for 40 years until the American version of the rule of thumb was overturned by a North Carolina court (although an appellate court upheld the rule of thumb three years later, in 1867). The right to chastise wives was finally overturned by courts in Alabama and Massachusetts in 1871. The state of Maryland was the first state to actually outlaw wife beating in 1883 (Davidson, 1978).

FAMILY VIOLENCE AROUND THE WORLD

Not only does conventional wisdom err when it argues that family violence is a modern phenomenon, it also errs when it asserts that private violence is unique to American families or, if not unique, that the problem is greater in the United States than in other societies.

Gathering information on family violence in other societies has proven difficult. Only the United States and Canada have specific legislation that requires the reporting of child abuse and neglect—thus there are no official report data on child or spousal abuse available in other nations (Kamerman, 1975). There have been few local, regional, or national surveys conducted on family violence in other

TABLE 2.1 Relationship Between Physical Punishment and Wife Beating

Wife Beating	Physical Punishment			
	Rare	*Infrequent*	*Frequent*	*Common*
Rare	Andamans Copper Eskimo Ifugao Iroquois Ona Thailand	Rural Irish Hopi Trobrianders		
Infrequent	Kanuri Lapps Lau Mataco Tucano	Klamath Masai Ojibwa Pymies Santal Taiwan Tikopia Tzeltal	Ashanti Cagaba Garo Pawanee Wolof	
Frequent	Bororo Iban Tarahumara	Kapauku Korea Kurd Toradja	Azande Dogon Somali	Amhara
Common	Chuckchee Tlingit Yanoama	Aymara Hausa	Ganda Truk	Serbs

SOURCE: Levinson (1981); reprinted with permission from *Child Abuse and Neglect*, 5, (4), David Levinson, "Physical punishment of children and wifebeating in cross-cultural perspective." Copyright © 1981, Pergamon Press, Ltd.

countries. Thus our comparisons of the level of intimate violence are largely based on clinical case data or data compiled by anthropologists.

The anthropologist David Levinson (1981) has examined the records of the Human Relations Area Files at Yale University. These records contain descriptive and statistical information on a wide range of societies over time and around the world. Levinson reports that wife beating is the most common and frequent form of family violence—thus confirming the theory that woman are generally considered the "most appropriate" victims of intimate violence (see Table 2.1).

Our own review of the available clinical and descriptive data indicates that family violence is most common in Western, industrialized, developed nations such as Great Britain, Germany, and France. Developing nations do report problems of violence and abuse. The apparent increase in abuse reports seems tied to the social disorganization that is occurring in these nations due to modernization. The People's Republic of China has frequently been described as a society with little or no child or wife abuse, although Westerners familiar with the patterns of child rearing in China 30 or 40 years ago doubt this claim.

Scandinavian countries are also described as having few problems with child abuse. This is generally thought to be due to social conditions being good, the widespread use of contraceptives limiting the number of unwanted children, free abortions, and the fact that working mothers can leave their children with day-care institutions (Vesterdal, 1977).

We tested the notion that Scandinavian countries have little problem with child abuse (Gelles & Edfeldt, 1986). Our colleague Åke Edfeldt, professor of education at the University of Stockholm, replicated our national survey of family violence. He translated the Conflict Tactics Scales into Swedish and conducted interviews with a nationally representative sample of 1,168 respondents who had children at home 3 to 17 years of age (this was essentially the same sampling approach we used in our 1976 national survey—Straus, Gelles, & Steinmetz, 1980).

The results of the comparison between the United States and Sweden were mixed. In general, the Swedish parents reported using less overall violence than did parents in the United States. However, when we confined our analysis to only the most severe and abusive forms of violence, there was no significant difference between the two countries. While differing social conditions may have played a role in limiting spankings, slaps, and other so-called minor acts of violence, parents in both countries are about equally likely to beat, kick, and punch their children.

Students of family violence around the world have tried to synthesize the various data that are available and come up with a general statement that explains why violence is common in some societies and rare in others. The anthropologist Jill Korbin (1981) concludes that, if children are valued for economic, spiritual, or psychological qualities, they are less likely to be maltreated. Certain children who are perceived to have undesirable qualities are at greatest risk of abuse. Thus illegitimate orphans, stepchildren, females, or retarded or deformed children are often at greatest risk of abuse. Some students of the new "one child" policy in the People's Republic of China note that an unintended consequence of the law to limit families to one child has been a rather dramatic increase in female infanticide (Korbin, 1981).

Rebecca and Russell Dobash (1979) also find that cultural values about women play a role in the risk of wife abuse. The more women are viewed as property of their mates, the greater the risk of abuse.

THE SOCIAL TRANSFORMATION OF FAMILY VIOLENCE

We have made the case that the problems of child abuse and wife abuse are not new. Nor are other forms of family violence—such as sibling violence and violence toward parents. Perhaps the only new form of family violence is the abuse of the elderly. This is essentially due to the increase in life expectancy—50 or 100 years ago people simply did not live long enough to become vulnerable to abuse at the hands of their middle-aged children.

Yet, although we find cases of family violence throughout recorded history, viewing family violence as a social issue and a social problem is a rather new phenomenon. For most of the time that there has been violence between loved ones, it has literally and figuratively occurred behind closed doors. It gradually became both a social issue—a condition that captures public attention and generates concern, controversy, and in some cases collective action—and a social problem—a condition found to be harmful to individual and/or societal well-being.

It is tempting to look for some dramatic change that took place 20 years ago that propelled family violence from behind closed doors into the public spotlight. That, however, would be naive. Violence in the home came to public attention gradually. The fortress doors of the private family did not swing open, they moved inch by inch over the decades.

Discovering Childhood and Children

The historical treatment of children is not entirely bleak. Children's rights were recognized, but slowly. In Mesopotamia, 6,000 years ago, children had a patron goddess to look after them. The Greeks and Romans had orphan homes. Some historical accounts also mention the existence of foster care for children. Samuel Radbill (1980) reports that child protection laws were legislated as long ago as 450 B.C., and at the same time the father's complete control over his children was modified. Anthropologists have noted that nearly every society has laws and rules regarding sexual access to children.

The social historian Phillipe Aries, in his book *Centuries of Childhood* (1962), claims that the concept of childhood as a distinct stage emerged after the Middle Ages. Before then, childhood as a stage ended when an infant was weaned. Children were seen as miniature adults and were portrayed as such in the artwork of the Middle Ages. Painting and sculpture of children pictured them with little heads and miniature adult bodies, dressed in adult clothing. Renaissance art was the first time children were portrayed as children.

Michael Robin (1982) has traced the roots of child protection. He found that the Renaissance was the beginning of a new morality regarding children. Children were seen as a dependent class in need of the protection of society. This was also a time when the family was looked to for teaching children the proper rules of behavior. At the same time, the power of the father increased dramatically.

While society paid more attention to children, this was not without some dire consequences. Puritan parents in colonial America were instructed by leaders such as Cotton Mather that strict discipline of children could not begin too early.

The Enlightenment in the eighteenth century brought children increased attention and services. The London Foundling Hospital was founded during the eighteenth century. The hospital not only provided pediatric care but, as Michael Robin (1982) recounts, was also the center of the moral reform movement on behalf of children.

In the United States the case of Mary Ellen Wilson is almost always singled out as the turning point in concern for children's welfare. Mary Ellen Wilson was an illegitimate child born in 1866 in New York City. Mary Ellen was in the care of foster parents when she was discovered beaten and neglected. Etta Wheeler was the charity worker who discovered Mary Ellen. Wheeler turned to the police and the New York City Department of Charities for help for Mary Ellen Wilson and was turned down—first by the police who said there was no proof of a crime and second by the charity agency who said they did not have custody of Mary Ellen. The legend goes on to note that Henry Berge, founder of the Society for the Prevention of Cruelty to Animals, intervened on behalf of Mary Ellen and the courts accepted the case because Mary Ellen was an animal. In reality, the court reviewed the case because the child needed protection. The case was argued, not by Henry Berge, but by his colleague, Elbridge Gerry.

Mary Ellen Wilson was removed from her foster home and placed in an orphanage. Her foster mother was imprisoned for a year, and the case received detailed press coverage for months. In December of 1874 the New York Society for the Prevention of Cruelty to Children was founded. Protective societies rose and fell during the next 80 years.

The political scientist Barbara Nelson (1984) notes that by the 1950s public interest in abuse and neglect was practically nonexistent. Technology paved the way for the rediscovery of child abuse. In 1946 the radiologist John Caffey (1946) reported on a number of cases of children who had multiple long bone fractures and subdural hematomas. Caffey used X rays to identify the fractures, although he did not speculate about the causes. P. V. Woolley and W. A. Evans (1955) did speculate that the injuries might be inflicted by the children's parents. Caffey (1957), writing in 1957, looked again at his X-ray data and speculated that such injuries could have been inflicted by parents or caretakers. By 1962, the physician C. Henry Kempe and his colleagues at the University of Colorado Medical Center (Kempe et al., 1962) were quite certain that many of the injuries they were seeing and the healed fractures that appeared on X rays were intentionally inflicted by parents.

Kempe's article became the benchmark of the public and professional rediscovery of child abuse. Kempe's article, and a strong editorial that accompanied it, created considerable public and professional concern. *Time, Newsweek, The Saturday Evening Post,* and *Life* followed up the Kempe article with news or feature stories. Barbara Nelson (1984) has traced the record of professional and mass media articles on child abuse and neglect. Prior to 1962 it was unusual that a single mass media article on abuse would be published in a year. After Kempe's article, there was a tenfold increase in popular articles that discussed child abuse. Today, a year does not go by without each major periodical publishing at least one story on child abuse. Kempe founded his own professional journal, *Child Abuse and Neglect: The*

International Journal, and thousands of professional articles are published annually in medical, sociology, psychology, social work, and other scholarly journals.

That public and professional media coverage of child abuse grew rapidly and in tandem was not a coincidence. Each professional journal article produced additional fodder for the mass media (many scholars and scholarly journals issue press releases to accompany publication of a new article). Each popular article added legitimacy to the public concern about abuse and stimulated a new round of research and scholarly publication.

The symbiotic relationship between scholarly and popular media was not without some problems. The translation of scientific writing into popular presentation often leveled, sharpened, and distorted the scientific findings and statements. For instance, the editorial that accompanied Kempe's article in the *Journal of the American Medical Association* said that "it is likely that [the battered-child syndrome] will be found to be a more frequent cause of death than such well recognized and thoroughly studied diseases as leukemia, cystic fibrosis and muscular dystrophy and might rank well above automobile accidents." By the time the statement in the editorial had found its way to the public press, it had been slightly changed to state that child abuse was one of the five leading causes of death of children. Similarly, estimates of the incidence of child abuse and the possible causes were stated and restated so often that they took on lives of their own—apart from the initial, speculative presentations in scholarly journals.

Two other forces worked to move child abuse out from behind closed doors during the 1960s. The first was the passage of child abuse reporting laws, and the second was the effort in the federal government to focus concern on the plight of abused children.

One of the concrete consequences of the rediscovery of child abuse after the publication of Kempe et al.'s 1962 article on the battered child syndrome was the passage of child abuse reporting laws in each of the 50 states between 1963 and 1967. Reporting laws were the quickest, most concrete measure states could take to demonstrate that they wanted to "do something" about the abuse of children. The underlying theme of many of the popular and professional publications on child abuse from the time of Mary Ellen Wilson was the fact that abused children were missing persons in social and criminal justice agencies. Many abused children came to public attention only at the point of death. Logic dictated that, if society were to help abused children, it would have to identify those in need of help. Not coincidentally, child abuse reporting laws were often viewed as a no- or low-cost means for state legislators to "do something" about abuse. Few legislators who jumped on the reporting law bandwagon could foresee that reporting laws would lead to uncovering hundreds of thousands of children who required state-funded protective services. The myth that family violence was rare had such a strong hold that most legislators assumed that the laws they passed would lead to uncovering only a handful of abused and neglected children in their states.

The Children's Bureau, first an agency in the Department of Labor, then an agency of the Department of Health, Education, and Welfare, was the first federal focal point of discussion and concern for abused children. The Children's Bureau was active in the cause of abused children as far back as the 1950s. The bureau was founded in 1912 by an act of Congress with the mandate of disseminating information on child development. The bureau also acquired the budget and mandate to conduct research on issues concerning child development. The Children's Bureau engaged in a variety of activities regarding child abuse and neglect. The agency participated in one of the earliest national meetings on child abuse sponsored by the Children's Division of the American Humane Association. After the publication of Kempe et al.'s 1962 article, the bureau convened a meeting to draft a model child abuse reporting law. The model law was drafted in 1963. Finally, the bureau funded a variety of research projects, including David Gil's first national survey of officially reported cases of child abuse. In 1974, Congress enacted the Child Abuse Prevention and Treatment Act and located the National Center on Child Abuse and Neglect in the Children's Bureau.

Congressional interest in child abuse prior to 1973 was limited to the passage of a reporting law for the District of Columbia and some attempts to pass national reporting laws. In 1973 then senator Walter Mondale introduced the Child Abuse Prevention and Treatment Act. Enacted in 1974, the act defined child abuse and neglect, established the National Center on Child Abuse and Neglect, set forth a budget for research and demonstration projects, and called for a national survey of the incidence of child abuse and neglect.

Child abuse appeared to be a "safe" congressional issue. Again, the myth that abuse was rare and confined to the mentally disturbed seemed to limit the scope of the problem and the need for large federal spending. Who could disagree, after seeing slides of horribly abused children, that such children did not need care and protection? Mondale needed a "safe" issue. He had seen his Comprehensive Child Development Act vetoed by then president Nixon. Even Nixon, Mondale would say, could not be in favor of child abuse.

Child abuse was not as "safe" an issue as it first seemed. One witness, Jolly K., a former child abuser and founder of Parents Anonymous, captured media and congressional attention with her testimony recounting her abuse of her child. But another witness, the social welfare expert David Gil, showed the "unsafe" side of the issue when he insisted on linking abuse to poverty. Moreover, Gil went beyond the narrow scope of the public stereotype of child abuse and introduced the issue of corporal punishment and spanking into his testimony. Finally, Gil concluded that the bill as written was too narrow to identify, treat, and prevent the real problem.

The Child Abuse Prevention and Treatment Act passed. It was never clear whether President Nixon could be against child abuse—he signed the bill in the midst of mounting public clamor over Watergate. The final amount of money made available for research and demonstration projects was small, $85 million. Many child abuse experts who realized how extensive the problem was and how difficult it would be to treat suggested that such a trifling amount was but a rounding error at the Pentagon. Yet, despite concern over the scope of the legislation and the narrowness of the mandate of the law, the passage of the Child Abuse Prevention and Treatment Act succeeded in creating a federal presence and a federal bureaucracy that could serve as a focal point of public and professional awareness of child abuse and neglect.

Discovering Wife Abuse

There was no Mary Ellen for battered women. No technological breakthroughs such as pediatric radiology to uncover years of broken jaws and broken bones. No medical champion would capture public and professional attention in the way Henry Kempe had for battered children. There was no "Women's Bureau" in the federal government. And, initially, there was no powerful senator who used a congressional committee chairmanship as a bully pulpit to bring attention to the plight of battered women.

The discovery of wife abuse was a traditional grass-roots effort. Attention to the problem of wife battering came from women themselves. A women's center in the Chiswick section of London founded by Erin Pizzey became a refuge for victims of battering. Pizzey wrote the first book on wife abuse, *Scream Quietly or the Neighbors Will Hear* (1974), and produced a documentary movie of the same name. Both captured the attention of women in Europe and the United States. Women's groups began to organize safe houses or battered wife shelters as early as 1972 in the United States. The National Organization for Women created a task force to examine wife battering in 1975.

The results of research on wife abuse in the United States began to be published in 1973. Data on the extent of the problem, patterns of violence, factors associated with wife abuse, and other analyses were quickly seized on by those who believed that the abuse of women deserved the same place on the public agenda that child abuse had attained. As with child abuse, scholarly publications fed media articles and media articles fed public interest, which led to more research and professional attention.

Still, by the early 1980s public and professional interest in wife battering lagged far behind interest in child abuse. There were some congressional hearings on wife abuse and Congresswoman Barbara Milkulski introduced legislation for a National Domestic Violence Prevention and Treatment Act. A Federal Office of Domestic Violence was established in 1979 only to be closed in 1981.

Some progress was made in the mid-1980s. The National Domestic Violence Prevention and Treatment Act was passed into law, although spending from this legislation has been but a trickle. The U.S. Attorney General's Task Force on Family Violence held hearings across the country in 1984 and published its final report in September 1984 (U.S. Department of Justice, 1984a).

A Concern for Private Violence

It is tempting to give credit for the discovery of a social problem to a single great person. The field of child abuse and neglect certainly owes much to the late C. Henry Kempe. Walter Mondale was thought a hero by those concerned for child protection. Another point of view is that no single person, journal article, or piece of legislation propels a problem from obscurity onto the public agenda. Rather, an issue slowly and gradually becomes a public issue.

The great man and the slow social movement explanations of the social transformation of family violence are inadequate. Rather, a variety of social movements and social concerns combined in the late 1960s to create a climate where people were ready and willing to listen to those concerned with the victimization of women and children.

The assassinations of John F. Kennedy, Robert Kennedy, and Martin Luther King, Jr. focused public concern for violence. The focus led to the establishment of the President's Commission on the Causes and Prevention of Violence. The commission's national survey on attitudes and experience with violence produced invaluable data for researchers in the field of family violence.

The 1960s were also a period of violent social protest, and race riots, again focusing public concern on violence. The baby-boomers of the 1950s were teenagers in the 1960s and, as is the case for those 18 to 24 years of age, they engaged in innumerable acts of delinquency and violence, pushing up the national homicide, assault, and rape rates. The public believed that we were in the midst of an epidemic of violence. Fear of violent crime began to paralyze American society. The Figgie Report found that four out of ten Americans are afraid of being assaulted, robbed, raped, or murdered in their homes or on the streets where they live and work.

Concern for violence would not have meant much had it not occurred at the same time as we were undergoing a resurgence of both the women's and the children's movements. These existing social movements provided the forum, the workers, and the energy to collect, organize, and present information on private victimization. Existing national groups who lobbied on behalf of women and children made it easier to lobby for national and regional attention to the problems of the abuse of women and children.

A final necessary and sufficient piece that made the puzzle into a portrait of a problem was the research being carried out by social and behavioral scientists. Until there could be scientific data to shatter the myths of abuse, it was impossible to convince the public and legislators that family violence was a legitimate problem deserving of a continued place on the national agenda.

CONTEMPORARY ATTITUDES

Violence between family members has a historical tradition that goes back centuries and cuts across continents. It should come as no surprise that contemporary social scientists have proposed that, in the United States and many other countries, "the marriage license is a hitting license" (Straus, Gelles, & Steinmetz, 1980). Numerous surveys and situations emphasize the point that today in the United States many people believe that, under certain circumstances, it is perfectly appropriate for a husband to hit his wife. The parents who fail to hit their children are considered to be deviant, and not the parents who hit.

At the end of the 1960s the U.S. Commission on the Causes and Prevention of Violence carried out a study of violence in the United States. The primary reason for the study was to try and understand the causes of the tragic rash of assassinations and riots that plagued the country between 1963 and 1968. Along with the questions on public violence, the commission asked a number of questions about private violence. Among the conclusions was that about one-quarter of all adult men, and one in six adult women, said they could think of circumstances in which it would be all right for a husband to hit his wife or for the wife to hit her husband (Stark & McEvoy, 1970). The same survey found that 86% of those surveyed agreed that young people needed "strong" discipline. Of the sample 70% thought that it was important for a boy to have a few fistfights while he was growing up.

Fifteen years after the U.S. Commission on the Causes and Prevention of Violence conducted their research, the sociologists Murray Straus, Richard Gelles, and Suzanne Steinmetz carried out the first national survey on family violence. Their questions regarding people's attitudes toward violence in the home confirmed the findings from earlier research. Just under one in four wives and one in three husbands thought that a couple slapping one another was at least somewhat necessary, normal, and good (Straus, Gelles, & Steinmetz, 1980, p. 47). More than 70% of those questioned thought that slapping a 12-year-old child was either necessary, normal, or good.

Anecdotal accounts further underscore the widespread cultural approval of private violence. In 1964 a young woman named Kitty Genovese was returning home to her apartment in the Queens section of New York City. She was accosted and repeatedly stabbed by a man; and, while a number of her neighbors heard her screams for help and watched the assault from windows, no one called the police. The young woman's death led many people to conclude that American society was corrupt, because bystanders seemed too apathetic or unwilling to get involved in a homicide. However, upon closer examination, it was suggested that the apathy of Kitty Genovese's neighbors was not the result of their lack of concern, or the fact that they were immune to violence after years of watching television. Rather, many of the witnesses thought that they were seeing a man beating his wife, and that, after all, is a family matter.

In Worcester, Massachusetts, a district court judge still sits on the bench and tries an occasional wife abuse case despite the fact that he is a wife beater who misrepresented his behavior under oath during a divorce trial (D'Agostino, 1983).

Millions laughed (and still laugh) when Jackie Gleason would rant, "Alice, you're going to the moon," while shaking an angry fist at his television wife in the popular program *The Honeymooners*.

Fairy tales, folklore, and nursery rhymes are full of violence against children. Hansel and Gretel, before they were lured into the gingerbread house, had been abandoned by their parents to starve in the forest because money was scarce. Snow White was taken in the woods to be killed by the huntsman on the order of the wicked queen who was her stepmother. Mother Goose's "Old Woman Who Lived in a Shoe" beat her children soundly and sent them to bed. "Humpty Dumpty" is a thinly disguised metaphor for the fragility of children, and "Rock-a-Bye Baby," with the cradle falling from the tree, is not even thinly disguised.

SUMMING UP

The chapters that follow document the extent of intimate violence in the United States today, consider the factors that are associated with acts of family violence, examine the various theories that have been brought to bear to explain violence in the home, and finally consider methods of treating and preventing family violence. The tragic nature of family violence and the emotions that are stirred up as a result of specific instances of child, wife, or elder abuse frequently focus our attention on the immediate situation or on a specific case. It is important to keep in mind that what we are experiencing is neither new nor particularly unique to our own society. While we look for causes and solutions in individuals, or families, or even in communities, we should remember that cultural attitudes about women, children, and the elderly, and cultural attitudes about violence as a means of self-expression and solving problems, are at the root of private violence.

We will see that income, stress, and other social-psychological factors are related to acts and patterns of domestic violence, but we need to consider that people have choices as to how they will respond to stress, crisis, and unhappiness, and the historical and cultural legacy of violence in the home is a powerful means of influencing what choices people consider appropriate. The sociologists David Owens and Murray Straus (1975) found that experience with violence as a child is one of the most powerful contributors to attitudes that approve of interpersonal violence. We now turn to an examination of violence toward children.

DISCUSSION QUESTIONS

(1) Why are women considered the "appropriate" victims of family violence?

(2) Identify the problems that hamper our ability to compare the extent of family violence in other Western and non-Western societies with the extent of family violence in the United States.

(3) What factors explain why violence toward children is common in some societies and rare in others?

SUGGESTED ASSIGNMENTS

(1) Read the Old and New Testaments of the Bible and identify examples of family violence (implicit or explicit).

(2) Read some Mother Goose nursery rhymes and identify themes or messages that seem to condone violence and abuse of children. Find other children's stories or fables that convey the same message.

(3) Watch Saturday morning cartoon shows and count how many violent acts are included per 10-minute segment.

CHAPTER 2

The Youngest Victims:
Violence Toward Children

SUE WAS A SINGLE PARENT who lived in a fourth-floor walk-up apartment. Her husband had left her three years earlier, and child support payments stopped within weeks of the final divorce decree. Poverty and illness were as much a part of Sue's home as the busy activity of her 4-year-old daughter Nancy. One cold gray March afternoon, Sue took Nancy out for a walk. Together they hiked up the steep pedestrian walkway of a suspension bridge that rose up behind their apartment. At the top of the bridge, Sue hugged Nancy and then threw her off the bridge. Sue jumped a moment later.

Miraculously, both Nancy and Sue survived. Both were plucked from the icy water by a fishing boat. Nancy, with major internal injuries, was rushed to a nearby hospital, and Sue, remarkably without major injury, was sped to a different hospital. Nancy joined the thousands of children each year who are admitted to hospitals for child abuse. Her case, and that of her mother, was starkly clear. An intentional act designed to grossly injure, harm, or kill a child. The child abuse team at the hospital that admitted Nancy had little trouble diagnosing Nancy's condition and immediately filed both a child abuse report and a restraining act that would keep Sue from removing Nancy from the hospital. When, after six months, Nancy was ready to be released, the hospital's attorneys filed a petition to terminate Sue's parental rights. The attorneys argued that Nancy would be best placed in a foster home or institution rather than being given to a relative (they suspected that there was considerable violence in the homes of Nancy's grandparents and aunts and uncles).

Few would question that Nancy was an abused child. Few would question the wisdom of the hospital in taking steps to assure that Nancy would be protected from further violence and injury. The case of Sue and Nancy (not their real names, and a composite of a number of child abuse cases) is unusual. It is unusual because the intent of the parent and the cause of the injury were so obvious. It is not the normal case that a hospital child abuse diagnostic team, or a team of social workers, has clear evidence about how an injury to a child occurred. More common is the case of a child who is observed at school or in a hospital emergency room with a cut, a broken bone, or some other injury. Physical examinations, interviews with the child and the parent, and an examination of the child's medical history (if available) can sometimes help unravel the case and separate true accidents from inflicted injuries. When a child experiences violence that does not produce a black or blue mark, cut, or injury, determining whether the child has been harmed is even more complex, because variable community standards and definitions of abuse have to be applied to an act that has produced no gross visible harm.

Determining the extent of child abuse and violence toward children in the United States is a difficult task because not all cases of abuse and violence are as obvious as that of Nancy and Sue. Estimates of the incidence of abuse vary, as do definitions and community standards. This chapter begins by reviewing various sources of information on the extent and nature of violence and abuse toward children. Before considering who abuses children, we consider the process by which child abuse is recognized and reported in the United States. Official reports of child abuse often misrepresent who the most likely abusers are, and, consequently, relying on these reports leads to the perpetuation of some of the myths we discussed in Chapter 1 (e.g., only poor people abuse their children). Finally, the chapter reviews the evidence on the consequences of child abuse.

THE EXTENT OF
VIOLENCE AND MALTREATMENT

Physical Punishment

Spanking children is perhaps the most common form of family violence in the United States, and because it is considered so appropriate, most people would object to calling it a case of family violence. Nevertheless, the main objective of a spanking or slapping of a child is to teach the child a lesson, to get the child to stop a certain behavior (running into the street, touching a hot stove), or to relieve a parent's own pent-up frustration. As we saw in the previous chapter, many parents feel that children *need* to be hit. Justifications from a number of parents illustrate this attitude:

> I spank her once a week—when she deserves it—usually when she is eating. I believe that a child should eat so much and that is it.

> Once in a great while I use a strap. I don't believe in hitting in the head or in the face—although, Rhoda, I slapped her in her face a couple of times because she was sassing. *That* she needed.

> But right now she doesn't understand that much. I mean you can't stand and explain really something in detail that she'll understand. So I slap sometimes. She understands when she gets a slap when she's done something wrong. (Gelles, 1974, pp. 62-63)

Of course, if the slight spanking or slap does not work, the parent will typically hit a little harder, at least until the child "gets the message."

> I used to use my hand—put them over my knee and give them a good swat. But then I got myself a little paddle—the ball broke off and I kept the paddle. (Gelles, 1974, p. 69)

Because the intent is to cause some slight harm so that the child will get the message, physical punishment, whether in the best interests of the child or not, is consistent with our definition of violence as described in Chapter 1. Social surveys indicate that physical punishment of children is used by 84% to 97% of all parents at some time in their children's lives (Blumberg, 1964; Bronfenbrenner, 1958; Erlanger, 1974; Stark & McEvoy, 1970).

Despite parents' descriptions of how and why they use violence, and the claim that physical punishment is used because parents cannot reason with very young children, physical punishment of children does not cease when the children are old enough to walk, talk, or reason with. Three studies of college and university students found that half were hit when they were seniors in high school (Mulligan, 1977; Steinmetz, 1971; Straus, 1971). The most recent of these studies reported that 8% of the students questioned reported that they had been "physically injured" by their parents during the last year they lived at home before entering college.[1]

Child Abuse

Various techniques have been used in attempts to achieve an accurate estimate of child abuse in the United States. In 1967, David Gil (1970) conducted a nationwide inventory of reported cases of child abuse (which, however, was before all 50 states had enacted mandatory reporting laws). He found 6,000 confirmed cases of child abuse. Gil also reported on an opinion survey that asked a representative sample of 1,520 adults if they had personal knowledge of families where incidents of child abuse had occurred: 45, or 3% of the sample, reported knowledge of 48 different incidents. Extrapolating this number to a national population of 110 million adults, Gil estimated that between 2.53 and 4.07 million children were abused each year, or between 13.3 and 21.4 incidents of abuse per 1,000 persons in the United States. Gil's data were later analyzed by Richard Light (1974) to correct for possible instances where the same abusive incidents were known by more than one person (Light assumed that if one adult in a household knew about the incident, then other household members might also know). Light's refined estimate was that there were 500,000 abused children in the United States during the year Gil conducted his survey.

Other investigators have tried to estimate how many children are physically abused by their parents. Nagi (1975) surveyed community agencies that have contact with abused children. He estimated that 167,000 cases of abuse are reported annually, while an additional 91,000 cases go unreported. Nagi estimated that there are 950,000 reportable cases of abuse and neglect each year—two-thirds of which are reported, and one-third of which are not. Vincent DeFrancis, then with the American Humane Association, testified before the U.S. Senate in 1973 and estimated that there are 30,000 to 40,000 truly abused children in the United States. Physician Vincent Fontana (1973) placed the figures as high as 1.5 million.

Studies of reported child maltreatment. As you can see, there seems to be a "guesstimate" of the extent of child abuse for every guesser. Two programs of research on reported and recognized child maltreatment shed some scientific light on how common abuse is. Although the studies were different in method, purpose, and findings, they do agree that abuse is considerably more common than people in the 1960s and even the 1970s believed.

TABLE 3.1 Estimated Number of Recognized In-Scope Children (per 1,000 per year)[a]

Form of Maltreatment and Severity of Injury/Impairment	Number of In-Scope Children	Incidence Rate
Form of Maltreatment:		
total, all maltreated children	1,025,900	16.3
total, all abused children	580,400	9.2
physical abuse	311,200	4.9
sexual abuse	138,000	2.2
emotional abuse	174,400	2.8
total, all neglected children	498,000	7.9
physical neglect	182,100	2.9
emotional neglect	52,200	0.8
educational neglect	291,100	4.6
Severity of child's injury/impairment:		
fatal	1,100	0.02
serious	157,100	2.5
moderate	740,000	11.7
probable	127,800	2.0

a. National incidence estimates by major form of maltreatment and by severity of maltreatment-related injury or impairments.

b. Totals may be lower than sum of categories, because a child may have experienced more than one in-scope category of maltreatment.

SOURCE: National Center on Child Abuse and Neglect (1988, tables 3-2, 3-3, and 3-4).

The National Center on Child Abuse and Neglect has conducted two surveys designed to measure the national incidence of reported and recognized child maltreatment (Burgdorf, 1980; National Center on Child Abuse and Neglect, 1988). Both surveys assessed how many cases were known to investigatory agencies and how many cases were known to professionals in schools, hospitals, and other social service agencies. Table 3.1 presents the results of the 1988 national incidence survey. A total of 1,025,900 maltreated children were known by the agencies surveyed in the study. Stated in terms of incidence rates, it was estimated that 16.3 children are abused and/or neglected annually for each 1,000 children in the United States younger than 18. Now, 16.3 per 1,000 might not seem like much, but keep in mind that, when statistics on crime are published, those estimates speak of incidence per 100,000 individuals. Child abuse is common enough to talk in terms of 1,000 children!

A second source of data on the extent of child abuse comes from the National Study of Child Neglect and Abuse Reporting conducted each year by the American Association for Protecting Children, a division of the American Humane Association. This annual study measures the number of families, alleged perpetrators, and children involved in official reports of child maltreatment; determines the source of the reports and their geographic distribution; describes the characteristics of families involved in official reports; and identifies and describes trends in the reporting data within states (American Association for Protecting Children, 1989). The data come to the American Association for Protecting Children from the individual states.

During 1987, 2,178,384 children were reported to state agencies for suspected child abuse and neglect, or 34.02 reports per 1,000 children in the United States. Of these, it is estimated that 686,000 reports were substantiated by state child protective service agencies.

There are problems with both studies of reported child maltreatment. First, definitions of maltreatment—including physical abuse—and reporting practices vary from state to state and from agency to agency. Each profession has a somewhat different definition of child abuse. Second, individual, agency, and state participation in the surveys is variable. Some states provide complete data to the American Association for Protecting Children while other states do not even participate. The national survey of cases that were known by professionals also had problems with some agencies fully cooperating and others failing to take part or providing only the most meager help.

National surveys of family violence. A source of data *not based* only on official reports or official awareness, but limited to only one aspect of child maltreatment—physical violence—are the surveys carried out in 1976 and again in 1985 by Murray Straus and Richard Gelles (Gelles & Straus, 1987, 1988; Straus & Gelles, 1986; Straus, Gelles, & Steinmetz, 1980). Straus and Gelles conducted two studies on the subject of family violence using nationally representative samples of 2,146 individual family members in 1976 and 6,002 family members in 1985. One part of the study focused on homes where children under the age

TABLE 3.2 Frequency of Parental Violence Toward Children

	Percentage of Occurrences in Past Year				Percentage of Occurrences Ever Reported
Violent Behavior	Once	Twice	More Than Twice	Total	
Threw something at child	1.5	.7	.9	3.1	4.5
Pushed, grabbed, or shoved child	5.8	7.5	14.9	28.2	33.6
Slapped or spanked child	8.1	8.5	39.1	55.7	74.6
Kicked, bit, or hit with fist	.7	.5	.3	1.5	2.1
Hit or tried to hit child with something	2.4	2.0	5.3	9.7	14.4
Beat up child	.3	.1	.2	.6	1.0
Burned or scalded child	.2	.1	.1	.4	.6
Threatened child with knife or gun	.1	.1	0	.2	.3
Used a knife or gun	.1	.1	0	.2	.2

SOURCE: Second National Family Violence Survey (Richard J. Gelles and Murray A. Straus, 1988).

of 18 years of age lived. Parents in these homes were asked to report on their own "conflict tactics techniques" with their children. Among the list of conflict tactics were nine items that dealt with physical violence. These items ranged from pushing and shoving to the use of a knife or gun (see Table 3.2 for a list of the violence items). The milder forms of violence were, of course, the most common. However, even with the severe forms of violence, the rates were surprisingly high:

- 1.5% of the parents reported that they kick, bite, or punch their child each year, while 2% of those surveyed said they have done these acts at least once while the child was growing up;
- slightly fewer than 1% of the parents said they beat their child at least once a year, while 1% said they had beaten their child;

- two children in 1,000 faced a parent who threatened to use a gun or a knife during the survey year; and
- three children in 1,000 were threatened with a weapon by a parent while growing up (about the same percentages held for children whose parents reported actually using a weapon).

Straus and Gelles (1988) also estimated the extent of abusive violence. Abusive violence was defined as acts that had a high probability of injuring the child (see Chapter 1 of this book). These included kicking, biting, punching, hitting or trying to hit a child with an object, beating up a child, burning or scalding, and threatening or using a gun or a knife:

- slightly more than 2 parents in 100 (2.3%) engaged in one act of abusive violence during the year prior to the survey, and
- 7 children in 1,000 were hurt as a result of an act of violence directed at them by a parent in the previous year.

Projecting the rate of abusive violence (2.3 per 100) to all children under the age of 18 years of age who live in the home means that 1.5 million children experience acts of abusive physical violence each year. Projecting the rate of injury (7 per 1,000) means that about 450,000 children are injured each year as a result of parental violence.

Acts of violence not only affect a large number of children, but on average they happen more than once a year. Straus and Gelles found that even the extreme forms of parental violence occur periodically and even regularly in the families where they occur. The median number of occurrences of acts of abusive violence was 4.5 times per year.

Straus and Gelles's study of violence toward children confirmed previous findings that violence does not end when the children grow up. More than 80% of the 3- to 9-year-olds were hit at least once a year (Wauchope & Straus, 1990). Two-thirds of the preteens and young teenagers were hit, and more than one-third of 15- to 17-year-olds were hit each year. Abusive acts of violence show no particular pattern with regard to age.

One of the important limitations to the survey conducted by Straus and his associates is that the survey measured only self-reports of violence toward children. Thus the results indicate the rates of violence admitted to by parents, not the true level of violence toward children. In addition, the actual measure of violence and abuse was confined to a small number of violent acts. Sexual abuse and other forms of maltreatment were not measured in the study.

Nevertheless, the national study did yield valuable information regarding violence toward children and a projection of a rate of child abuse that was considerably higher than most other estimates of reported physical abuse. This is quite remarkable when one considers that Straus and his colleagues used a rather restricted list of abusive violent acts.

Child Homicide

Homicide is one of the five leading causes of death for children between the ages of 1 and 18 years of age. Even with an estimate this high, researchers believe that homicides of infants are probably underrecorded in health statistics (Jason, Gilliland, & Tyler, 1983). Homicides may be misrecorded as accidents either because the medical examiner is unable to verify the exact cause of death or because the medical examiner wants to protect the family as a result of their status and position in the community. Between 1976 and 1979 there were 7,026 children who were recognized as victims of homicide. Of the 178 neonates (newborns) who were killed, 66% were killed by a parent, 1% by a stepparent, and 2% by another family member. Infants (from 1 week to 1 year of age) were most likely to be killed by a parent (72%). Stepparents accounted for 2% of the homicides, while other family members accounted for 4%. The pattern changes for older children. Of the homicides of children 1 to 17 years of age, 23% were perpetrated by parents, 3% by stepparents, and 6% by other family members (Jason, Carpenter, & Tyler, 1983). The most recent data, according to statistics collected by the National Committee for Prevention of Child Abuse, indicate that there were 1,225 child maltreatment-related fatalities in 1988 (Mitchel, 1989).

Is Child Abuse Increasing?

Since the early 1960s there has been a widespread belief that the rates of child abuse and violence toward children have been increasing. This belief has been partially supported by the fact that the number of cases of child abuse that are reported to social service agencies has been rising at a rate of about 10% each year since 1983 (American Association for Protecting Children, 1989). Data collected by the American Association for Protecting Children (1989) show that, overall, there has been a 225% increase in child maltreatment reporting between 1976 and 1987. The largest yearly increase was from the first year of the study (1976) to the next year—an increase of 24.2%. The rate of change fell to 4.4% in 1987.

As we noted earlier, the National Center on Child Abuse and Neglect has conducted two national surveys of the incidence of reported and recognized child abuse and neglect. The most recent survey found that countable cases of child maltreatment that have come to the attention of community professionals increased 66% over the number of cases found in 1980. There were significant increases in the incidence of physical and sexual abuse, with physical abuse increasing by 58% and sexual abuse more than tripling between 1980 and 1986.

Straus and Gelles (1986) analyzed data from the Second National Family Violence Survey and found that parent reports of physical child abuse had *declined* 47% between 1975 and 1985, from 36 per 1,000 to 19 per 1,000 children. The rate of abusive violence toward Black children increased, but the change was not statistically significant (Hampton, Gelles, & Harrop, 1989). One possible explanation for the decrease in self-reports of violence toward children is that parents are becoming less candid because of the unacceptability of admitting to abusive behavior. Straus and Gelles (1986) recognized that changing attitudes about child abuse could be a plausible explanation for their findings. They also note, however, that the declining rate of child abuse is consistent with the changing character and structure of the American family, the improving economy, increased publicity about child abuse, and the rapid expansion of treatment and prevention programs for child abuse. The American family has become smaller in the last decade. Individuals are getting married later in life, having children later, having fewer children, and having fewer unwanted children. All these factors are consistent with lower risk of violence toward children. In addition, both the inflation rate and the rate of unemployment declined between 1975 and 1985. Given the expansion of both public awareness of child abuse and treatment and prevention

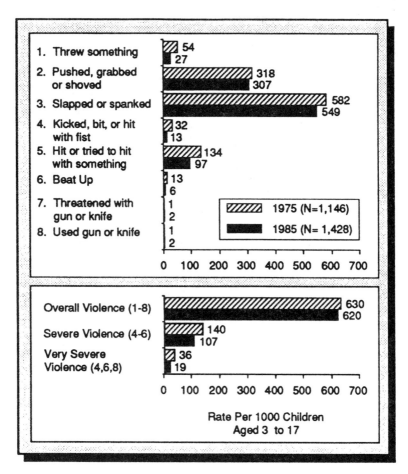

Figure 3.1: Parent-to-Child Violence: Comparison of Rates in 1975 and 1985

programs, it would have been surprising and depressing to find that the rate of violence and abuse had increased.

Straus and Gelles attempt to resolve the apparent contradiction between their surveys and the results of the studies of officially reported and recognized child maltreatment. They note that an increase in the official report rate is not necessarily contradictory with a decline in the incidence rate. It is possible, Straus and Gelles explain, that an increase in the former (which is a proxy for the number of cases of abuse that are treated) could very well produce a decline in the latter.

WHO ARE THE ABUSERS/
WHO IS ABUSED?

There are three sources of information about who abuses children and which children are the most likely to be abused. Each source of information has specific strengths and weaknesses. Sometimes the information from each source conflicts, while, other times, the findings are quite consistent. To be able to appreciate the claims and findings from each source, it is important to assess the relative strengths and weaknesses of the major types of information we have on the factors associated with child abuse.

A major source of information about child abuse is clinical studies. Clinical studies depend on information collected by clinicians such as social workers, psychiatrists, psychologists, and marriage counselors. Clinicians can collect a considerable range of data with much detail because the clinicians see their patients over a period of time. However, clinical data typically are based on only a few cases (clinicians can only see a certain number of patients a week), and these cases are not randomly or representatively selected. Consequently, although data from clinical studies may be rich in descriptive information, one cannot generalize from these small numbers of cases to any larger population. Another limitation is that clinicians typically do not compare the information they obtain from cases of abuse with information from other families where abuse does not occur. Thus they cannot be sure that the factors they find in the abusive families are unique to or even associated with the acts of abuse.

A second source of information about child abuse is official reports. The American Association for Protecting Children is a clearinghouse for official reports, as we mentioned in the previous section. Also, each state has its own official reporting system and records. Official reports provide information about a large number of cases and describe a wide range of cases of abuse. However, the data speak more to the factors that lead someone to get reported for abuse than to what factors are actually associated with child abuse. There is a tendency for lower-income and lower-social-status individuals (e.g., Blacks, Spanish-speaking, ethnic minorities) to be overrepresented in these reports. Child abuse researchers have found considerable bias in the process of officially labeling and reporting child abuse. The physician Eli Newberger and his associates (1977) report that lower-class and minority children seen with injuries in a private hospital are more likely than middle- and upper-class children to be labeled abused. Patrick Turbett and Richard O'Toole (1980), using an experimental design, found that physicians are more likely to label minority children and lower-class children as abused (a mock case was presented to the physicians, with the injury remaining constant and the race or class of the child varied).

The third source of information is survey data collected from representative samples of a given population. Unfortunately, there have been very few surveys conducted on child abuse. Two such studies are the ones conducted by Murray Straus and Richard Gelles (Gelles & Straus, 1988; Straus, Gelles, & Steinmetz, 1980).

Our discussion of factors associated with child abuse draws from all three sources of information. Where the three sources agree, we find the most powerful explanations of what child factors and parent factors are related to the abuse of children.

Child Factors

The very youngest children appear to be at the greatest risk of being abused (Fergusson, Fleming, & O'Neil, 1972; Gil, 1970; Johnson, 1974). Not only are young children physically more fragile and thus more susceptible to injury, their vulnerability makes them more likely to be reported and diagnosed as abused when injured. Older children are underreported as victims of abuse. Adolescent victims may be considered delinquent or ungovernable, and thus thought of as contributing to their own victimization.

Younger boys are more likely to be abused than older boys. The national survey of reported child abuse found that older girls were more likely to be victimized than younger girls (Straus, Gelles, & Steinmetz, 1980).

Early research suggested that there were a number of factors that raise the risk of a child being abused. Low-birth-weight babies (Parke & Collmer, 1975), premature children (Elmer, 1967; Newberger et al., 1977; Parke & Collmer, 1975; Steele & Pollock, 1974), and handicapped, retarded, or developmentally disabled children (Friedrich & Boriskin, 1976; Gil, 1970; Steinmetz, 1978b) were all described as being at greater risk of being abused by their parents or caretakers. However, a recent review of studies that examine the child's role in abuse calls into question many of these findings (Starr, 1988). One major problem is that few investigators used matched comparison groups. Second, newer studies fail to find premature or handicapped children being at higher risk for abuse (Egeland & Vaughan, 1981; Starr, Dietrich, Fishoff, Ceresine, & Demorest, 1984).

Parent Factors

Individual traits. Some clinical studies suggest that parents who score low on intelligence tests are more likely to abuse their children (Smith, Hansen, & Noble, 1973; Wright, 1971). However, most students of child abuse have found little difference between abusers and nonabusers in terms of intellectual ability (see, for example, Starr, 1982).

As we discussed in the first chapter, a consistent finding in early clinical studies of abuse was that mental illness and psychosis were common among abusers. Numerous personality characteristics have been related to abuse, including depression, immaturity, and impulsiveness. However, no consistent personality profile of abusers has emerged from the years of research on child abuse, and some researchers believe that what personality factors are found tend to be associated with being labeled an abuser rather than actually being related to abuse.

Another pervasive notion is that alcohol or drug misuse is associated with abuse (Fontana, 1973; Martin & Walters, 1982; Wertham, 1972; Young, 1964). A recent review of the relationship between alcohol, alcohol abuse, and child abuse concluded that, if alcohol is involved in child abuse, its influence does not appear to be strong nor pervasive but restricted to certain subgroups of abusers or types of abuse (Leonard & Jacob, 1988). Other researchers note that alcohol probably plays no direct role in abuse; rather, drinking and drunkenness can be used as a socially acceptable excuse for mistreating children (Gelles, 1974; Straus, Gelles, & Steinmetz, 1980).

A final individual factor sometimes found in abusive parents is that they tend to have unrealistically high expectations for their children. It is not uncommon for a 6-month-old infant to be admitted into a hospital for injuries inflicted by a parent who was angry because the child was not toilet trained. Research results, however, are inconsistent and it does not appear that abusive parents are markedly deviant in their knowledge of children's normal developmental milestones (Starr, 1988).

Family factors. Single parents and stepparents have been thought to be at high risk of abusing their children. Official report data and survey data show that single parents are overrepresented among abusers (American Humane Association, 1984; Gelles, 1989; Sack, Mason, & Higgins, 1985; Wilson, Daly, & Weghorst, 1980). Two explanations have been offered for why single parents are more likely to abuse their children. First, single parents often have to meet the demands of child rearing without the assistance of another adult. Second, single parents are more likely to live in poverty than dual caretaker couples. Our own analysis of the data from the Second National Family Violence Survey found that single parents were more likely to hit and abuse their children. The greater risk was not a function of single parents having to raise their children alone--single parents alone had the same rates of violence and abuse as single parents who lived with other adults. The risk of violence in single parent homes was a function of the high rate of poverty that single parents—mostly single mothers—must endure (Gelles, 1989).

The wicked stepparent is a staple of children's literature, and students of child abuse have often found stepparents to be over-represented in clinical and official report data on child maltreatment (American Humane Association, 1976; Daly & Wilson, 1980, 1981, 1985, 1987, 1988; Gil, 1970; Giles-Sims & Finkelhor, 1984; Wilson & Daly, 1987). Survey data, however, do not support the claim that stepparents are more violent or abusive than genetic parents (Gelles & Harrop, 1989).

It is generally thought that the risk of child abuse was highest in families with the largest number of children (Starr, 1988). Our own survey found that the rate of abuse was higher in two-child families than in one-child homes. The rate peaked in homes with five children. However, the rate of abuse was actually lowest in the largest families (Straus, Gelles, & Straus, 1980). We noted that this may be due to older children being able to help with child care and other household responsibilities in homes with seven or eight children.

Demographic Factors

Clinical, official reports, and survey data show that mothers are more likely to abuse their children than fathers. Although the difference between men and women is not large, what difference does exist is probably due to factors other than gender. Mothers tend to spend more time with children, especially younger children and infants. Irrespective of the time actually spent with children, in our society mothers are considered more responsible for the children's behavior than fathers. The most recent national survey of family violence found no difference between mothers' and fathers' use of violence toward their children (Wauchope & Straus, 1990). And young adults are more likely to abuse their children than older parents (American Humane Association, 1980; Gil, 1970; Lauer, 1974; Straus, Gelles, & Straus, 1980).

Official reports of child abuse overrepresent Blacks in comparison with the percentage of Blacks in the general population; although the national survey of the incidence of reported and recognized child maltreatment found that the rates of maltreatment among Blacks were no greater than the rates among other racial groups (Burgdorf, 1980). Ten years ago the First National Family Violence Survey found that the rates of violence and abuse were essentially the same in Black and White families (Straus, Gelles, & Straus, 1980). In 1985 the rate of overall violence remained the same in Black and White homes, but the rate of abusive violence toward Black children was about twice the rate for abusive violence toward White children (Hampton, Gelles, & Harrop, 1989).

Economic Factors

Clinical, official reports, and survey data are consistent in the finding that economic factors are significantly related to abuse. Low-income families have the highest rates of physical abuse and the abuse is the most likely to be reported. Those in the lowest-income groups have two or three times greater rates of abuse than upper-income families. Again, it is important to remember that abuse does occur in all economic groups, but it is *most likely* to happen among the poor or disadvantaged.

Because income is related to abuse, we should not be surprised that other socioeconomic factors are also related. A person's occupation has a significant impact on the chances of abuse occurring. Blue-collar workers have higher rates of the use of physical punishment and abuse (Kohn, 1977; Straus, Gelles, & Steinmetz, 1980; Steinmetz, 1971). Children whose fathers are unemployed or work part-time are more likely to be abused compared with children of fathers with full-time jobs. There was a time when some child abuse researchers thought that working mothers were more likely to abuse their children. However, research finds that whether a mother works or does not work has no direct impact on her chances of abusing her child (Gelles & Hargreaves, 1981).

Stress

Given that poverty and unemployment are linked to violence toward children, it is also likely that other forms of personal and family stress are associated with violence and abuse. Stressful situations such as a new baby, presence of a handicapped person in the home, illness, death of a family member, and child care problems are all found to be linked to higher rates of abuse and violence. Poor housing conditions and larger than average family size are also risk factors for maltreatment of children (Gil, 1970; Johnson & Morse, 1968; Straus, Gelles, & Steinmetz, 1980).

Social Isolation

Parents who abuse their children tend to be socially isolated from both formal and informal social networks (Elmer, 1967; Garbarino & Gilliam, 1980). Smith (1975) found that abusive mothers have fewer contacts with their parents, relatives, neighbors, or friends and they engaged in few social or recreational activities. When parents are not engaged in a social network, they lack social support during times of stress. Moreover, they are less likely to change their behavior to conform with community values and standards (Steinmetz, 1978b). Thus they are particularly vulnerable to responding violently to stress and not seeing this behavior as inappropriate.

The Cycle of Violence

No finding in the child abuse and violence toward children literature has been more consistently reported than the finding that persons who observed family violence, were victims of violence, or were exposed to high levels of family violence in childhood are more likely to be abusers (Elmer, 1967; Straus, Gelles, & Steinmetz, 1980; Wasserman, 1967). We have already provided the caution that this does not mean that all victims of childhood violence will grow up to be abusers, nor are people who have no violence in their childhood experience immune to violent behavior as adults. Joan Kaufman and Edward Zigler (1987) reviewed the empirical literature that tested the theory of the cycle of violence (also referred to as the "intergenerational transmission of violence hypothesis"). Kaufman and Zigler report that most papers on this topic still base the observations on case studies of children treated in hospital emergency rooms. A second source of data is agency record studies, which, according to Kaufman and Zigler, have limited value for testing the cycle of violence hypothesis. The third source is self-report studies.

Reviewing the self-report studies that examined the cycle of violence hypothesis, Kaufman and Zigler found that the rate of intergenerational transmission ranged from 18% to 70%. They conclude that the best estimate of the rate of intergenerational transmission appears to be 30% (plus or minus 5%). Based on this estimate, Kaufman and Zigler (1987) conclude that it is time for the intergenerational myth to be set aside and for researchers to cease asking, "Do abused children become abusive parents?" and ask, instead, "Under what conditions is the transmission of abuse likely to occur?"

Kaufman and Zigler's (1987) conclusion appears to be as sweeping and unsupportable as the claim that *all* abused children will grow up to be abusive. While the best estimate of rate of 30% intergenerational transmission is quite a bit less than half of abused children, the rate is considerably more than the between 2% and 4% rate of abuse found in the general population.

Three recent studies provide some of the better data on the cycle of violence theory. Rosemary Hunter and her colleagues (Hunter, Kilstrom, Kraybill, & Loda, 1978) studied mothers of premature or ill newborns and found that 10 out of their sample of 255 were reported for substantiated incidents of abuse or neglect during the first year of life. Nine of the ten mothers reported a family history of abuse, whereas only 17% of the comparison mothers reported such a history. Of the 49 families in which a parent reported being abused as a child, 9 parents abused their infants (Hunter & Kilstrom, 1979). Byron Egeland, Deborah Jacobvitz, and L. Alan Sroufe (1988) note that this rate will increase as the infants are followed beyond the first year.

Byron Egeland and his colleagues (Egeland, Jacobvitz, & Papatola, 1987; Egeland, Jacobvitz, & Sroufe, 1988) have conducted a prospective study of the intergenerational transmission of violence. They followed a sample of 160 high-risk, low-income mothers. In this prospective study, 70% of the parents who were identified independently as having experienced child abuse were observed to maltreat or provide borderline care. In the most recent report of this survey, Egeland, Jacobvitz, and Sroufe (1988) report that those mothers who were able to break the cycle of violence were significantly more likely to have received emotional support from a nonabusive adult during childhood, participated in therapy during any period in their lives, and had a nonabusive, more stable, emotionally supportive and satisfying relationship with a mate.

A third study conducted by Ellen Herrenkohl, Roy Herrenkohl, and Lori Toedler (1983) found that 47% of the parents who were abused as children abused their own children. This percentage is significantly higher than the percentage for the nonabused parents.

In summary, there have only been a few controlled studies that actually test the public perception that abused children grow up to be abusive parents. Most studies conclude that the majority of abused children do not go on to be abusive parents. However, a violent background is an important contributor to the *likelihood* that a person will be violent toward a child.

Summary

From the preceding discussion of factors that are associated with violence toward children and child abuse, it should be quite clear that there is no single factor that leads a parent to abuse a child. Characteristics of the child, parent, family, social situation, and community are related to which children are abused and under what conditions. Figure 3.2 summarizes the factors in a social-psychological model of child abuse. This summary should not be confused with a causal explanation of violence and abuse. Chapter 6 will review the theories and explanation of family violence in detail.

We can safely say at this point that there are multiple causes of child abuse. Because there are multiple causes, rather than a single cause, this has a profound effect on the process of identifying and treating abuse. Obviously, a clinical assessment of suspected abuse cannot

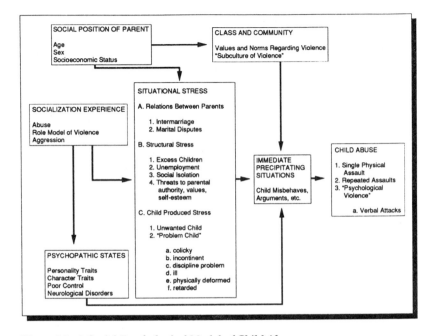

Figure 3.2: A Social-Psychological Model of Child Abuse
SOURCE: Gelles (1973); reprinted with permission from the *American Journal of Orthopsychiatry*. 1973 by the American Orthopsychiatric Association, Inc.

simply look for a single factor to signal whether a child has been abused. It is not sufficient to know that the parents were abused. An assessment of only one parent will not be sufficient; neither will an examination of just the parent's home and life-style be sufficient. Many a social worker has misdiagnosed a suspected injury by relying too much on whether or not the child's home was neat. As we will see in the concluding chapter of this book, prevention and treatment need to be based on a model of multiple causes. The needs of the child, parents, family, and social situation are all important in understanding and helping the abusive family.

CONSEQUENCES OF CHILD ABUSE

The child abuse literature contains many assumptions about the consequences of violence and abuse for the victim, his or her family, and the society. The immediate, tragic consequences are the injuries experienced by the victim. Death is another sad and tragic consequence of abuse in hundreds of homes a year.

The consequences of violence and abuse may extend beyond the victim and beyond the home. Some researchers believe that untreated abused children frequently grow up to be delinquents, murderers, and batterers of the next generation of children (Schmitt & Kempe, 1975). Survey research supports some of the findings from the clinical literature. A study of 4,465 children and their siblings who were reported to be victims of maltreatment in eight counties in New York State found that the maltreated children had higher rates of involvement in the juvenile justice system (Alfaro, 1977; Carr, 1977). Cathy Spatz Widom (1989) identified a large sample of validated cases of child abuse and neglect from approximately 20 years ago, established a control group of nonabused children, and assessed official arrest records to establish occurrences of delinquency, criminal behavior, and violent criminal behavior. She reports that abused and neglected children have a higher likelihood of arrest for delinquency, adult criminality, and violent criminal behavior than the matched controls. The results, she explains, provide strong support for the cycle of violence hypothesis.

Abused children have frequently been described as having a number of cognitive, emotional, and social difficulties (Starr, 1988). Recent research indicates that children who experience the more severe forms of maltreatment suffer more significant intellectual deficits (Dietrich, Starr, & Weisfeld, 1983). Other studies find various social and emotional deficits, including communication problems, poor performance in school, and learning disabilities (Starr, 1988). As adults, abused children are also thought to have higher rates of drug and alcohol abuse, criminal behavior, and psychiatric disturbances (Smith, Honigsberg, & Smith, 1973). Society also pays a price for abuse and violence toward children. Many murderers and assassins experienced violent childhoods. Arthur Bremer, who attempted to assassinate Alabama's Governor George Wallace, wrote in his diary, "My mother must have thought I was a canoe, she paddled me so much" (Button, 1973).

In summary, the legacy of child abuse is more than the physical scars that children carry with them. Research indicates that there are emotional and developmental scars as well. Family violence can also spill out onto the street. Moreover, there is the issue of quality of life—the day-to-day impact of violence and its threat to children and the entire family.

NOTE

1. All the studies of college students used "convenience" or accidental samples. Questionnaires were filled out by students enrolled in introductory sociology or psychology classes. Because the samples were not representative, the results cannot be generalized to the campuses where the research was done. Because college students are not representative of all eighteen year olds, the results cannot be generalized to all high school seniors. Nevertheless, the results from a number of different campuses are quite consistent, and suggest that even in fairly affluent, White middle-class homes, violence toward children extends well into children's adolescence.

DISCUSSION QUESTIONS

(1) What techniques have been used to measure the extent of child abuse in the United States? Discuss the advantages and disadvantages of each technique.
(2) Are poor people more likely to abuse their children, to be correctly or incorrectly labeled "child abusers," or both?
(3) For clinicians who must diagnose and treat child abuse, what are the implications of the conclusion that there are multiple factors associated with the abuse of children?

SUGGESTED ASSIGNMENTS

(1) Observe how parents discipline children in a public place. Develop a "coding" form by which you can keep track of how frequently parents use physical punishment to discipline their children. Try to observe in different locations and see whether the setting, situation, and social class of the parents influences their public behavior.
(2) Contact your local child welfare agency (state, city, or local). Ask for the official tally of child abuse reports for the last 10 or even 20 years. See whether you can see any trends in the changes.

CHAPTER
4
The "Appropriate" Victims: Women

THE SCENE IS THE emergency room of a major children's hospital. This evening, like so many before, and so many that would follow, the staff is hovering over a suspected case of child abuse. A 3-year-old boy is being examined. He has a number of cuts and abrasions, but what catches everyone's attention is the outline of a hand on the side of his face. A young intern suddenly turns to the boy's mother and yells at her. "How could you do this?" he begins, until he finally concludes, "I will see that your child is taken away from you and this will never happen again!"

The senior social worker on duty moves in and takes the young physician aside. Beginning with the obvious statement, "You seem to be upset," the social worker then asks the intern if he can describe the mother. "Tell me what she looks like," the social worker asks. The physician, a little calmer, could offer only the briefest description. "Come back with me," the social worker offers, and they return again to the mother and the child. "How did you lose your front teeth?" the social worker asks the mother. "Oh, my husband knocked them out last week," the mother replies in a flat, emotionless tone. Turning to the intern, the social worker notes, "You have two victims here."

Wife abuse was publicly recognized as a social problem some 10 years after child abuse had received widespread public attention. And yet women are still overlooked as victims of family violence, by both physicians and the public. There is no federally funded national center for wife abuse (although there was a short-lived Center on Domestic Violence in the federal government in the late 1970s). Few states have passed official reporting laws for wife abuse, although many states have revised their family and criminal laws to deal with wife battery. No national clearinghouse exists for collecting data on cases of wife abuse or spousal violence. Women who are abused are generally ignored or treated less seriously than child victims of family violence. When asked why the U.S. Senate was not holding hearings on wife abuse, as it did for child abuse, a senator replied that eliminating wife abuse "would take all the fun out of marriage." A district court judge in an eastern city, after hearing a wife present her case against her husband's violence, leaned over the bench and smiled at the husband and said, "If I were you, I would have hit her too."

As we noted in Chapter 2, there are abundant historical and cross-cultural data to support the claim that women are the "appropriate victims" of domestic violence. In fact, some researchers have gone so far as to claim that the "marriage license is a hitting license." Lately, we have learned that it does not take a license to hit. This chapter begins by reviewing some of the newest research in the field of family violence, the study of courtship or dating violence. Next, we consider the extent of violence toward wives and what factors are associated with wife battery. The following section takes on the most pervasive myth in the study of wife abuse; if women stay with their assaultive husbands, then they, the women, must like the violence. In this section we review the reasons why some women stay in violent relationships and why others leave. We also examine research that looks at women who stayed with their husbands and got their husbands to stop the violence. Finally, the chapter concludes with a discussion of husbands as victims of domestic violence.

COURTSHIP VIOLENCE

The virtues of romantic love, a phenomenon considered synonymous with American dating patterns, have been extolled in poems, songs, romance novels, television soap operas, and folklore. Sadly, along with the moonlight cruises, the first kiss, the flirtations, and the affection is also the startling fact that violence is very much a part of American dating patterns. Studies that examined the possibility of violence in dating and courtship found that between 10% and 67% of dating relationships involve violence (Sugarman & Hotaling, 1989). As with other forms of intimate violence, the milder forms of violence (pushing, slapping, shoving) are the most common. However, severe violence is surprisingly common. Researchers have found that the rate of severe violence among dating couples ranged from about 1% each year to 27% (Arias, Samios, & O'Leary, 1987; Lane & Gwartney-Gibbs,

1985; Makepeace, 1983). This violence is also a pattern among couples of high school age: 12% of high school daters reported experiencing a form of dating violence (Henton, Cate, Koval, Lloyd, & Christopher, 1983). One victim reported having a gun or knife used on her, while two persons said they used a gun or a knife on a dating partner.

Perhaps the saddest and most revealing finding from the research on dating violence is how the individuals perceive the violence. In a study conducted by the sociologist June Henton and her colleagues (1983), more than one-fourth of the victims, and three of ten offenders, interpreted the violence as a sign of love. This is a scary extension of the elementary school yard scenario where the young girl recipient of a push, shove, or hit thinks that it means the boy who hit her likes her.

Perhaps the biggest surprise from the research on dating violence is that rather than the violent episodes shattering the romantic images held by the participants, one gets the impression that violence serves to protect the romantic illusions of dating. Victims of dating violence were likely to take the blame for helping to start the violence and were reluctant to blame their partners for the abuse. In addition, victims of courtship violence were reluctant to tell others about their experiences. If they did talk about the violence, it was with peers and not parents or teachers.

It is quite clear from the studies of courtship violence that many of the patterns we find in martial violence emerge long before a person gets married. One study, in which battered women who had sought shelter were interviewed, found that 51% of these women said that they had been physically abused in a dating relationship (Roscoe & Bernaske, 1985). If the marriage license is not a hitting license, then we must focus more closely on the relationship between romance, intimacy, and violence.

EXTENT OF MARITAL VIOLENCE

The pattern of courtship violence helps us to understand some important things about marital violence. First, as we have noted previously, there is a tendency on the part of many victims and offenders to view the violence as appropriate. Second, female victims are reluctant to blame their partners for the violence and tend to say that both persons were to blame for the abuse. Third, victims might blame themselves ("I asked for it"). Last, there is a tendency not to talk about the violence with family or friends.

Because violence between husbands and wives was traditionally hidden in the home, there has been a general lack of awareness of the seriousness and extent of the problem. Whereas mandatory reporting laws for child abuse and neglect were enacted in every state in the late 1960s and early 1970s, only three states have mandatory reporting laws for spouse violence. Some hospitals record the number of women treated for spousal violence, and most police departments keep a rough record of domestic disturbance calls. Even without official records on spouse abuse, a variety of data sources suggest that spouse violence is far more extensive than commonly realized.

Homicide

Homicide is the one aspect of spousal violence on which official data are available. Researchers generally report that intrafamilial homicides account for between 20% and 40% of all murders (Curtis, 1974). In 1984, 806 husbands were killed by their wives, while 1,310 wives were slain by their husbands (Federal Bureau of Investigation, 1985).

Criminal Assault

In one study, aggravated assault between husbands and wives made up 11% of all reported criminal assaults (Pittman & Handy, 1964). In another report, husband-wife assault constituted 52% of all assaults in Detroit (Boudouris, 1971). Because so many assaults are recorded as domestic disturbance calls, police reports surely underestimate the proportion of all assaults that are intrafamilial.

Applicants for Divorce

Studies of couples applying for divorce also provide some information on the extent of husband-wife violence. The psychologist George Levinger (1966) discovered that 22% of the middle-class and 40% of the working-class applicants for divorce whom he interviewed discussed "physical violence" as a major complaint. John O'Brien

(1971) reports that 17% of the couples he interviewed spontaneously mentioned violent behavior in their marriages.

National Crime Survey Report

Another source of information on the extent and patterns of domestic violence is the National Crime Survey, conducted by the U.S. Justice Department. This survey estimates the amount of crime committed both against persons aged 12 and older and against households. The chief advantage of the National Crime Survey is that it investigates the occurrence of crime whether it is reported to the authorities or not (the Uniform Crime Reports cited above only measure crimes reported to the police). The U.S. Bureau of Justice has published two reports on intimate violence based on data collected for the National Crime Survey. The first report, *Intimate Victims: A Study of Violence Among Friends and Relatives* (U.S. Department of Justice, 1980), reported on events occurring between 1973 and 1976 as derived from the interviews conducted twice a year with approximately 136,000 occupants of a representative sample of some 60,000 housing units in the United States.

The major findings from these interviews were as follows:

- There were about 3.8 million incidents of violence among intimates in the four-year period of the survey. Nearly a third were committed by offenders related to the victims.
- An analysis of single-offender incidents revealed 1,055,000 incidents between relatives. Of this number, 616,000 (58%) were between spouses or ex-spouses.

The second report, *Family Violence* (U.S. Department of Justice, 1984b), states:

- The yearly incidence of domestic violence among those 12 years of age or older was 1.5 per 1,000 people in the population.

A National Survey of Marital Violence

Although each of the pieces of information mentioned above offers a clue to the actual level of martial violence, the studies have numerous methodological flaws. Like the research on child abuse discussed in the previous chapter, studies of wife abuse and spousal violence frequently rely on small, nonrepresentative samples or the use of official data (e.g., police calls). It is impossible to generalize from these studies to marriage in the United States. The National Crime Victim survey failed to employ a precise measure of violence, and thus the results are rather difficult to interpret.

The same national studies that examined child abuse (see the previous chapter) also examined marital violence. Richard Gelles and Murray Straus interviewed a nationally representative sample of 2,143 family members in 1975 and a nationally representative sample of 6,002 individuals in 1986. Using the same Conflict Tactics Scale, the researchers examined violence between husbands and wives.

- In 16% of the homes surveyed in 1986, some kind of violence between spouses had occurred in the year prior to the survey. More than one in four (28%) of the couples reported marital violence at some point in their marriages.

As with violence toward children and courtship violence, the milder forms of violence were the most common (see Table 4.1):

- In terms of those acts of violence that would be considered wife beating (that is, had the high potential of causing an injury), the national family violence survey revealed that 3.4% of American women, or 1 woman in 22, was a victim of abusive violence during the 12-month period prior to the interview in 1986.

Wife beating is an unfortunate pattern, not a single event, in most violent households. On average, a woman who is a victim of wife abuse is abused three times each year.

Is Marital Violence Increasing?

Just as many people believe that child abuse is increasing, so too do people believe that violence between partners has increased. Data from the Second National Family Violence Survey (Straus & Gelles, 1986) indicate that the rate of wife abuse declined 21.8% from 1975 to 1985 (see Figure 4.1). This decline, while substantively large, was not

TABLE 4.1 Frequency of Marital Violence: Comparison of Husband and Wife Violence Rates (in percentages)

| | Incidence Rate | | Frequency | | | |
| | | | Mean | | Median | |
Violent Behavior	Husband	Wife	H	W	H	W
1. Threw something at spouse	2.9	4.6	3.7	2.7	1.5	1.0
2. Pushed, grabbed, or shoved spouse	9.6	9.1	2.9	3.1	2.0	2.0
3. Slapped spouse	3.1	4.4	2.8	2.7	1.0	1.0
4. Kicked, bit, or hit with fist	1.5	2.5	3.9	2.9	1.5	1.0
5. Hit or tired to hit spouse with something	1.9	3.1	3.6	3.3	1.2	1.1
6. Beat up spouse	.8	.5	4.2	5.7	2.0	2.0
7. Choked spouse	.7	.4	1.9	2.9	1.0	1.0
8. Threatened spouse with knife or gun	.4	.6	4.3	2.0	1.8	1.1
9. Used a knife or gun	.2	.2	18.6	12.9	1.5	4.0
Overall violence (1-9)	21.3	12.4	5.4	6.1	1.5	2.5
Wife-beating/husband-beating (4-9)	3.4	4.8	5.2	5.4	1.5	1.5

SOURCE: Second National Family Violence Survey (Richard J. Gelles and Murray A. Straus, 1988).

statistically significant. Wife abuse toward Black women declined 43%—and this decrease was statistically significant (Hampton, Gelles, & Harrop, 1989).

The rate of abusive violence toward husbands remained essentially unchanged in the general population. The rate did increase among Black men, but the difference was not statistically significant.

As with their analysis of changing rates of violence toward children, Straus and Gelles (1986) attribute the decline in violence toward women to changing attitudes about wife abuse, the changing character and structure of the American family, the improving economy, increased publicity about wife abuse, and the rapid expansion of treatment and prevention programs for battered women. Whereas

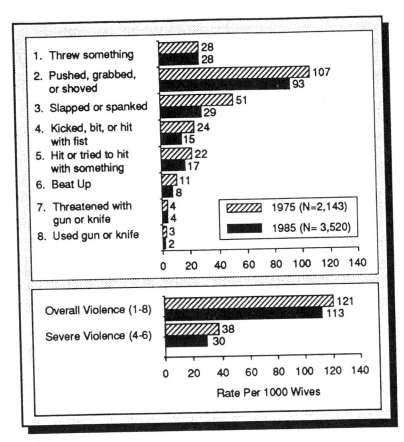

Figure 4.1: Husband-to-Wife Violence: Comparison of Rates in 1975 and 1985

there were but a handful of shelters for battered women in 1975, when the First National Family Violence Survey was conducted, there were more than 1,000 shelters in 1986. Other treatment programs have been developed, including peer counseling groups for violent men. There has also been a growth of paid employment for married women, and working women have narrowed the gap between their wages and the wages of men.

The lack of a change in the rate of violence toward men is possibly a result of the lack of attention and lack of programs for male victims of intimate violence. We will have more to say about this in the final section of this chapter.

A Note on Marital Rape

Just as violence is not the only form of abuse children experience, physical abuse is not the only form of victimization wives endure. The sociologist Diana Russell (1980) interviewed a representative sample of 930 women in San Francisco. Of the 644 married women in the sample, 12% said they had been raped by their own husbands. The sociologists David Finkelhor and Kirsti Yllö (1985) interviewed 323 Boston-area women for their book, *License to Rape: Sexual Abuse of Wives*; 10% of the women said they had been forced to have sex with their husbands or partners. Last, Richard Gelles and Murray Straus asked a nationally representative sample of women if their partners ever tried or forced them to have sexual relations by using physical force. The results indicate that 50 women per 1,000 have husbands who attempt to force them to have sex each year, while 80 women per 1,000 are forced to have sex by their husbands. These studies produce the same remarkable findings: One of the most common forms of sexual victimization for a woman is to be forced into having sex, or engaging in a sex act she objects to, by her husband. Russell found that twice as many women in her sample had been raped by their husbands as by strangers. Even these statistics are low, because many women do not see forced sex with a husband as rape.

FACTORS ASSOCIATED WITH WIFE ABUSE

The earliest publications on the subject of wife abuse took a distinctively psychiatric view of both offender and victim. Women who were abused were believed to suffer from psychological disorders, as were the men who abused them. Research conducted in the 1970s and 1980s found this view of wife battery too simplistic. There are a number of individual, demographic, relational, and situational factors related to violence toward wives. These factors are probably all interrelated. For example, certain relationship patterns are probably more common in certain social classes than others.

Individual Factors

Batterers. Men who assault and batter their wives have been found to have low self-esteem and vulnerable self-concepts. A remark, insult, or comment that might not affect someone else may be interpreted as a slight, insult, or challenge to many of these men. Abusive men have also been described as feeling helpless, powerless, and inadequate (Ball, 1977; Weitzman & Dreen, 1982). Wife beaters have been described as sadistic, passive-aggressive, addiction prone, pathologically jealous, pathologically passive, and dependent (Margolin, Sibner, & Gleberman, 1988). Gerald Hotaling and David Sugarman (1986) concluded that the picture of an assaultive man that has emerged in the literature is consistent with the diagnoses of Borderline and Antisocial Personality disorders. Violence is frequently used as a means of trying to demonstrate one's power and adequacy.

Abused women. Psychological portraits of battered wives are difficult to interpret. One never really knows whether the personality factors found in battered wives were present before they were battered or are the result of the victimization. As with other studies of family violence, personality studies of battered women frequently use small samples or clinical samples and often fail to have comparison groups. Thus generalizing from these studies is difficult, and demonstrating that battered women are actually different from nonvictimized women is nearly impossible using these data.

Battered women have been described as dependent, having low esteem, and feeling inadequate and helpless (Ball, 1977; Hilberman & Munson, 1977; Shainess, 1977; Walker, 1979). Descriptive and clinical accounts consistently report a high incidence of depression and anxiety among samples of battered women (Hilberman, 1980). Barbara Star and her colleagues' (1979) review of the battered wife literature concludes that the literature is "replete with reports of low self-esteem, depressive illnesses, suicide attempts, and characterological disorders among samples of battered women."

Sometimes the personality profiles of battered women reported in the literature seem directly opposite. While some researchers describe battered women as unassertive, shy, and reserved (Weitzman & Dreen, 1982), other reports picture battered women as aggressive, masculine, frigid, and masochistic (Ball, 1977; Snell, Rosenwald, & Robey, 1964).

It is best to be wary of psychological profiles of battered women. In addition to small samples and no comparison groups, samples of battered women are frequently drawn only from battered wife shelters. Thus the researchers are studying only one type of battered women, those who seek help, and it is certainly unrealistic to generalize from these women to all battered women. Second, it is likely that many of the personality factors found among samples of battered women are a consequence of being battered (Gelles & Harrop, 1989).

Alcohol. Studies of marital violence typically find a relationship between alcohol use and abuse and domestic violence. Various studies note that between 36% and 52% of wife batterers also abuse alcohol (Brekke & Saunders, 1982). Virtually every study of wife abuse conducted notes the close link between alcohol and violence (Leonard & Jacob, 1988). However, as we noted in Chapter 1, some research studies find that, although there is a strong relationship between alcohol and violence, physical violence in families actually declined when drunkenness occurred "almost always" (Coleman & Straus, 1983). Also, alcohol is not an immediate antecedent of violence in the majority of families in which violence occurs (Kantor & Straus, 1987).

That alcohol is related to wife abuse is clear. What is not clear is how alcohol is related to violence. Do men drink, lose control, and then abuse? Or does alcohol become a convenient excuse or rationalization for violent behavior? Cross-cultural studies of alcohol use and studies of marital violence suggest that alcohol itself does not lead to violence; rather, men drink (or say they drink) to have a socially acceptable excuse for violent behavior (Gelles, 1974).

Demographic Factors

Results of the National Family Violence Survey indicate that all forms of marital violence occur most frequently among those under 30 years of age (Straus, Gelles, & Steinmetz, 1980). The rate of marital violence among those under 30 years of age is more than double the rate for the next older age group (31 to 50). Studies that examine women who seek help from agencies or shelters also find that the mean age is 30 or younger (Fagan, Stewart, & Stewart, 1983; Gayford, 1975).

Straus and his colleagues also found that wife abuse was more common in Black households than in White households. Obviously, race is not the only factor in play here. Income and occupational status are probably also associated with the increased rates of wife abuse among Blacks.

Marital violence can occur at any stage of a marriage, but as the data on age would appear to indicate, newer marriages have the highest risk of wife abuse. Maria Roy found that the highest percentage of battered women were married from 2.5 to 5 years (1977). Another study reported that the median length of a violent marriage was 5 years (Fagan, Stewart, & Stewart, 1983).

Economic Factors

Irrespective of the method, sample, or research design, studies of marital violence support the hypothesis that spousal violence is more likely to occur in low-income, low-socioeconomic-status families. These findings do not mean that wife abuse is confined only to low-income, low-status families. One woman who was married to a *Fortune* 500 corporate executive described how her husband beat her and how, in order to escape his violence, she slept in their Continental Mark IV every Saturday night. A good deal of violence in middle- and upper-class families is kept secret. Neighbors do not live close by and do not call the police. Upper-class husbands seem to have more success in keeping the police from arresting them. Nevertheless, it would appear that the probability of wife abuse occurring in high-income, upper-class homes is less than the probability of its occurrence among the poor.

One of the main factors associated with wife battery is the employment status of the husband. Being unemployed is devastating to men in our society. It is a clear demonstration that they are not fulfilling society's expectation that men should be the family providers. Unemployed men have rates of wife assault that are almost double the rates for employed men (Gayford, 1975; Prescott & Letko, 1977; Rounsaville, 1978). Men who are employed part-time have even higher rates, probably because they have the worst of all possible worlds—no full-time job and ineligible for unemployment or other benefits (Straus, Gelles, & Straus, 1980).

The Cycle of Violence

As with child battering, wife battering is related to experiences with violence. Men who have experienced violent childhoods are more likely to grow up and assault their wives than are individuals who have not experienced childhood violence. The physician J. J. Gayford (1975), as well as other investigators, has found that both offender and victim had violence-ridden childhoods (Fagan, Stewart, & Stewart, 1983; Roy, 1977). Studies also find that observing parental violence is related to spousal aggression (Pagelow, 1981; Rosenbaum & O'Leary, 1981). This finding is consistent for men: Those who observe their parents use violence are much more likely to grow up to be abusive partners. The evidence for women is inconsistent and it is not clear whether women who observe their parents' violence are likely to become violent adults (O'Leary, 1988).

Again, it is *very* important to introduce the caution that a violent background does not predetermine a violent adulthood. Although the chances of being an offender and victim are increased if one grows up in a violent home, there are many violent people who had limited exposure to violence as children, and some people who experienced extremely violent childhoods grow up to be nonviolent.

Relationship Factors

One of the most compelling indicators that domestic violence is not purely a product of individual pathology is the finding that certain properties of marital relations raise the likelihood of violence. That structural properties of marriage and family life are involved means that abuse cannot be solely attributed to "bad" or "sick" people.

Early studies of spousal violence found that men whose educational attainment and occupational status were lower than their wives were more likely to assault their wives than men who were better educated and had better jobs than their spouses (Gelles, 1974; O'Brien, 1971). Additional research bears out the hypothesis that status inconsistency and status incompatibility are related to marital violence. One example of status inconsistency is when a husband's educational background is considerably higher than his occupational attainment (e.g., a Ph.D. who drives a taxicab). "Status incompatibility" describes the situation where the husband, who society expects to be the leader of the family, has less education and a poorer job than his wife. In both of these cases, the risk of marital violence is elevated (Hornung, McCullough, & Sugimoto, 1981; Rounsaville, 1978; Steinmetz, 1978b).

Decision-making patterns, or power balance, was also found to be related to domestic violence. Families in democratic households—homes where the decision making is shared—are the least violent (see Figure 4.2). Homes where all the decisions are made either by the wife or the husband have the highest rates of violence.

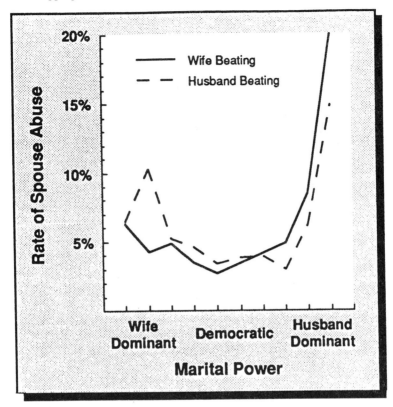

Figure 4.2: Marital Violence by Marital Power
SOURCE: From Straus, Gelles, and Steinmetz (1980).

There is a final relationship factor: If there is one type of family violence in a home, there is a good chance that another form of violence will be present. Child abuse rates are higher in homes where there is spouse abuse (Finkelhor, 1983; Hilberman & Munson, 1977; Straus, Gelles, & Steinmetz, 1980).

Stress and Isolation

Social stress and social isolation are two final factors that are strongly related to the risk of wife abuse. Unemployment, financial problems, sexual difficulties, low job satisfaction, large family size, and poor housing conditions are all related to marital violence. The more socially isolated a family is, the higher the risk that there will be wife abuse.

STAYING IN OR LEAVING
BATTERING RELATIONSHIPS

One thing is quite clear from the review of research on wife abuse—violence in marital relationships is not a one-shot affair but a pattern that endures over a considerable period of time. Because marital violence is a recurrent behavior, and because the victims— women—are adults and not helpless children, some people have assumed that the solution to marital violence is for the battered women to leave or divorce their husbands. We noted in Chapter 1 that one of the most pervasive myths in the field of family violence is the myth that battered wives like being hit, otherwise they would leave. Considerable research has been conducted that refutes the myth of the masochistic battered wife. In general the studies find that many factors—economic, relational, cultural, and social—constrain women from leaving a battering relationship.

The psychologist Lenore Walker (1979) has examined numerous cases of battered women and has developed the theory of "learned helplessness" to explain why so many women endure such extreme violence for so long. Walker notes that women who experience re-peated physical assaults at the hands of their husbands have much lower self-concepts than women whose marriages are free from vio-lence. Walker postulates that the repeated beatings and lower self-concepts leave women with the feeling that they cannot control what will happen to them. They feel they are unable to protect themselves from further assaults and feel incapable of controlling the events that go on around them. Thus, like laboratory animals, which, after expe-riencing repeated shocks from which there is no apparent escape, battered women eventually learn that they are helpless to prevent violent attacks.

"Learned helplessness" implies a rather passive nature in battered women, and it is important not to confuse the situation of women who are battered with the situation of the laboratory animals from whom the theory of "learned helplessness" was derived. As we will see from the research we will review shortly, most battered women are far from passive. They call the police, they go to social workers or mental health agencies, they flee to shelters or the homes of friends or parents, and they fight back. But, in many ways, women are constrained by social forces from permanently leaving a violent relationship. Legal writer Elizabeth Truninger (1971) lists seven factors that help explain why women do not break off relationships with abusive husbands: (a) they (the women) have negative self-concepts, (b) they believe their husbands will reform, (c) there is economic hardship, (d) they have children who need a father's economic support, (e) they doubt they can get along alone, (f) they believe divorcees are stigmatized, and (g) it is difficult for women with children to get work.

In our own research we compared battered women who stayed with their violent husbands with women who called the police, sought a divorce, or went to a mental health agency for help. We found that certain factors distinguished women who stayed in the violent relationship from women who sought help or left a violent husband. First, those women who leave seem to experience the most severe and frequent violence. Second, women who experienced more violence as children were more likely to remain in violent relationships. In addition, women with limited educational attainment and occupational skills were more likely to stay with battering husbands. The fewer resources a woman had, the less power she had, the more she was entrapped in a marriage, and the more she suffered at the hands of her husband (Gelles, 1976).

The sociologist Millie Pagelow (1981) has also investigated the situation of battered women. Her research on women who sought help from shelters confirms some of our findings while other findings are not supported in Pagelow's study. Pagelow administered questionnaires to 350 women who had sought temporary residence for themselves or their children in battered wife shelters. Severity and frequency of violence did not influence the decision of whether or not to leave. While some of the women in the shelters endured years of violence and abuse, others fled after the first or second incident. Also, Pagelow did not find support for the association between violence experienced as a child and the decision to stay or leave. Actually, shelter residents who experienced childhood violence were more apt to leave after the first incident of violence or else they remained in a violent home a shorter time than other women. Pagelow did find that the resources women had (education, occupation, income) did influence whether they stayed or left a violent husband.

The sociologists Michael Strube and Linda Barbour (1983) talked with 98 battered wives and also confirmed that economically dependent women were more likely to remain with an abusive husband. They also found that wives who stayed with violent men reported they were more "committed" to the marital relationship.

In contrast to studies of women who leave their husbands, the sociologist Lee Bowker examined the stories and situations of women who chose to stay with their husbands and got them to stop being violent. Bowker (1983) conducted 136 in-depth interviews over a nine-month period with women who stayed with their husbands and succeeded in getting their husbands to stop using violence. Bowker used a variety of strategies to locate these women—referrals from social service agencies, radio and television appearances by members of the research team, newspaper advertisements, and so on.

Bowker learned that the techniques used by women to get their husbands to stop using violence clustered into three types: (a) personal strategies, including talking, promising, threatening, hiding, passive defense, aggressive defense, and avoidance; (b) use of informal help sources, including family members, in-laws, neighbors, friends, and shelters; and (c) formal help sources, including the police, social service agencies, and lawyers and district attorneys. The most common personal strategy was passive defense—covering one's body with arms, hands, or feet. The most common informal strategy was friends; social services were the leading formal source of help.

Which technique worked best? There was no simple answer. Bowker reports that no single strategy is guaranteed to stop violence, but almost any strategy or help source can ultimately work. What matters is "the woman's showing her determination that the violence must stop now."

We used the opportunity of our Second National Family Violence Survey to extend the research carried out by Lee Bowker. Whereas he advertised for a small sample of women in Milwaukee, we had access to more than 3,000 women representative of the entire population of married women, women living with men, or women recently divorced (Gelles & Straus, 1988). Shock, surprise, and the stunning realization that a woman was hit by someone she loves probably explains why crying was the immediate response to violence most frequently reported. Many women reacted more actively. The second most common immediate response was yelling and cursing at a violent spouse. Nearly one in four victims (24%) hit their attacker back—despite the obvious risks of escalating the violence. It is not surprising that those women who were victims of severe violence were somewhat more reluctant to hit their husbands back than were the victims of minor violence. Immediately seeking help from the police was the least likely response, especially for victims of minor violence. Fewer than 3% of the victims of minor violence immediately called the police after they were attacked, while five times that percentage (14%) of the victims of beatings, choking, and other forms of severe violence immediately called the police. After we talked with victims of intimate violence about their immediate reactions to being hit, we turned our attention to the more deliberate and long-term steps taken by assaulted women to get their husbands or partners to stop hurting or threatening them. The single most common strategy that victims used to attempt to prevent future violence was avoiding their spouses and staying away from certain topics of conversation. The second most common long-range prevention strategy was trying to talk husbands out of being violent. The women who use the talking strategy generally try to use logic and rational discussion and argument to persuade husbands to stop being violent. We found that the third most widely used mechanism for attempting to limit violence was hiding or leaving. In just the last year before we interviewed them, nearly all of the battered wives (seven out of ten) had left their assaultive spouses. Keeping in mind that these are women who had been battered for a number of years, it is reasonable to assume that every one of them left for some period of time during the course of the battering.

We also asked women to assess the effectiveness of the strategies they used. Just as Lee Bowker discovered, the most effective strategy for stopping wife beating was a woman's conviction and determination that the violence must stop now. The single most effective strategy employed by the national sample of women was persuading husbands to promise not to be violent again. The least effective strategy was hitting back.

A NOTE ON HUSBANDS AS VICTIMS

The results of the Second National Family Violence Survey (summarized in Table 4.1) include data on violence toward husbands. A little more than 4% (4.4%) of the wives surveyed reported that they

had engaged in violence toward their husbands that could be considered abusive (Gelles & Straus, 1988). Violence toward husbands, or
"husband abuse," has been a controversial area in the study of domestic violence. There has been considerable rhetoric on this topic, but,
unfortunately, precious little scientific data.

In 1978, the sociologist Suzanne Steinmetz published an article
designed to demonstrate that husbands as well as wives were the
victims of violence in the home. Steinmetz reviewed numerous investigations of family violence and found, contrary to some feminist and
scholarly claims, women were not the *only* victims of family violence.
Steinmetz went on to claim that it was husband and *not* wife abuse
that was the most underreported form of family violence. Steinmetz
was immediately challenged and attacked by feminists and scholars
alike for misreading, misinterpreting, and misrepresenting her findings (see Pleck, Pleck, Grossman, & Bart, 1978).

Unlike most debates among scholars, this one spilled over into the
public media (*Time,* the *Today* show, the *Donahue* show, *The David
Susskind Show*) and even into the syndicated column of Ann Landers
(for a detailed discussion of the public debate, see Jones, 1980). Sadly,
the debate boiled in the public domain, but the issue received virtually
no attention in the scholarly arena. Few scholarly articles on violence
toward husbands have been published since Steinmetz's article in
1978, although there was another heated exchange on husband abuse
in the 1980s (McNeeley & Robinson-Simpson, 1987; and letters to the
editor in *Social Work,* Vol. 33, pp. 189-191, 1988).

It is quite clear that men are struck by their wives. It is also clear
that because men are typically larger than their wives and usually
have more social resources at their command, that they do not have
as much physical or social damage inflicted on them as is inflicted on
women. Data from studies of households where the police intervened
in domestic violence clearly indicate that men are rarely the victims
of "battery" (Berk, Newton, & Berk, 1983). Thus, although the data in
Table 4.1 show similar rates of hitting, when injury is considered,
marital violence is primarily a problem of victimized women.

DISCUSSION QUESTIONS

(1) Compare the nature of courtship violence with that in marriage. Is the
marriage license a hitting license or are there other factors that increase
the risk that intimates will be violent toward one another?

(2) Discuss the various ways economic factors influence the chances that spouse abuse will occur.

(3) Why is it unfair to "blame" battered women for remaining with their battering spouses? What resources or facilities in the community could help women who wanted to leave their violent husbands?

(4) Are there battered husbands?

SUGGESTED ASSIGNMENTS

(1) Identify the services that exist for battered women in your community (e.g., shelters or safe houses, hot lines, counseling groups for battered women, and so on).

(2) Talk to someone who works in a shelter or a safe house. Is the address of the shelter public or a secret? How many women and children can the shelter hold? Does the shelter ever turn away women? Why? What is the philosophy of the shelter—how do they approach the problem of violence toward women?

(3) Create a resource book for victims of spouse abuse in your community—include the names, addresses, and telephone numbers of all resources that could be used by victims of spouse abuse.

(4) Find out what services (if any) are available for victims of courtship violence at your college or university.

Hidden Victims: Siblings, Adolescents, Parents, and the Elderly

THE INCREASING PUBLIC AND professional attention paid to child and wife abuse has had the unanticipated consequence of leading many people to believe that violence toward women and children is the most common and most problematic aspect of violence in the home. Yet, children and women are not the only victims of family violence. In fact, they are not the most commonly victimized family members—siblings are.

This chapter examines violent family relations that have been largely overlooked by the public, researchers, and members of the social service and public policy communities. Each form of violence has been overlooked for a slightly different reason. Violence between siblings is so common that people rarely think of these events as family violence. We have already mentioned adolescent victims of family violence when we discussed violence toward children (see Chapter 3). Discussions of child abuse rarely extend beyond the youngest victims. Older victims of parental violence tend to be blamed for their own victimization. Teenagers are thought of as causing their own victimization, and, as we blame the victim, we tend to overlook this violent family relationship. Parent abuse is considered almost humorous by those who first hear of it. Researchers who study parent abuse have been teased that they must be running out of victims or asked if "pet abuse" is next on their list. The large majority of parent victims are so shamed by their victimization that they are reluctant to discuss anything but the most severe incidents; and, when they do report, they, like adolescent victims, are blamed for being hit. Finally, the elderly are victims of intimate violence. They may be truly the hidden victims, because one of the unfortunate aspects of aging in our society is the removal of the elderly from their regular and normal systems of social interaction (e.g., work).

Although research on most of these types of family violence is scarce (there has been an increase in research on elder abuse in the last few years), any book on family violence would be incomplete without a discussion of violent relations other than parent to child and between husband and wife.

SIBLING VIOLENCE

Normative Attitudes Toward Sibling Violence

Sibling violence is the most common form of family violence. Siblings hitting one another is so common that few people consider these behaviors violent. The existence of social norms that encourage expressions of aggressive behavior among siblings hinders the recognition of sibling violence as abnormal and worthy of serious concern. Most parents view conflict among siblings as an inevitable part of growing up and rarely discourage expressions of aggressive behavior between their offspring. However, as the sociologist Suzanne Steinmetz (1987) notes, our complacency about sibling violence needs to be reexamined in light of statistics that indicate that in Philadelphia between 1948 and 1952 and in New York in 1965, 3% of all homicides were sibling homicides (Bard, 1971; Wolfgang, 1958).

Sociologists who have studied violence between brothers and sisters have found that parents feel it is important for their children to learn how to handle themselves in violent situations. Parents do not actively discourage their children from becoming involved in disputes with their siblings. In fact, parents may try to ignore aggressive interactions and only become involved when minor situations are perceived as escalating into major confrontations. Sibling rivalry is considered a "normal" part of relations between brothers and sisters, and many parents believe that such rivalry provides a good training ground for the successful management of aggressive behavior in the real world. American parents generally feel that some exposure to aggression is a positive experience that should occur early in life. Seven out of ten Americans agreed with the statement: "When a boy is growing up it is important for him to have a few fist fights" (Stark & McEvoy, 1970). And the better prepared children are to defend themselves against a sibling, the better prepared they will be for conflicts with classmates and friends.

The sociologist Suzanne Steinmetz (1977), in her study of sibling conflict in a representative sample of 57 intact families in Delaware, found that it was sometimes difficult to get parents to discuss sibling violence, not because they were ashamed or embarrassed to admit such behavior, but because the parents often did not view their children's actions as abusive and worthy of mentioning. When questioned further about particular incidents, parents said that they found their children's conduct to be annoying but they did not perceive the situation as one of conflict. When prompted, parents will freely discuss or admit the existence of sibling violence in their homes. Parents willingly tell friends, neighbors, and researchers, without embarrassment or restraint, how their children are constantly involved in argumentative and abusive behavior toward one another. When Steinmetz asked the parents in her study: "How do your children get along," she received such statements as:

> Terrible! They fight all the time.
> Oh it's just constant, but I understand that this is normal.
> I talk to other people and their children are the same way. (Steinmetz, 1977, p. 43)

From these typical comments, it becomes obvious that parents view such frequent and violent confrontations as inevitable.

Perhaps parents may be somewhat justified in their assessment of the inevitability of sibling violence. The existence of sibling rivalry has been documented throughout history. Researchers, pointing to the historical existence of sibling rivalry, refer to the biblical story of Cain and Abel, in which Cain kills his brother (Sargent, 1962; Straus, Gelles, & Steinmetz, 1980). This is perhaps the earliest, although certainly not the only, recorded account of sibling violence. Evidence of violence between brothers and sisters can also be found in more contemporary sources. However, what is lacking in the recorded accounts of sibling violence is information from controlled, scientific research projects. The sociologists Suzanne Steinmetz and Murray Straus report that, prior to their own investigations into the causes, frequency, and patterns of sibling violence, information on noninfant, nonfatal sibling violence was almost nonexistent.

Those research articles that did appear in the scientific literature prior to 1977 dealt almost exclusively with sibling murders (Adelson, 1972; Bender, 1959; Sargent, 1962; Smith, 1965). Society appears only to take notice of the most extreme expressions of sibling violence. Levels of violence among siblings that do not exceed the levels defined as socially acceptable or "normal" go unnoticed by both researchers and society in general. This historic acceptance of sibling violence as normal and inevitable has made it difficult to establish whether the rates of sibling violence have increased, decreased, or remained the same. Baseline data simply do not exist. Even today, after the completion of a few studies on sibling violence, the level of awareness concerning sibling violence as a significant form of family violence is low.

The Extent of Violence Between Siblings

Steinmetz's (1977) previously mentioned investigation into sibling rivalry discovered frequent occurrences of sibling conflict in American families. The parents in 49 families recorded the frequency and types of violent behavior occurring between their offspring during a one-week period. Steinmetz reported that a total of 131 sibling conflicts occurred during this period, ranging from short-lived arguments to more serious confrontations. She believes, however, that this figure, although high, is probably a considerable underestimation of the true extent of sibling aggression. She notes that there are many problems inherent in relying upon parents to record the frequency of sibling conflicts. For example, in most of the families in Steinmetz's sample both parents worked, reducing the amount of time the parents actually spent with their children. This in turn reduced the opportunity of parents to observe and record violent behaviors between children. Steinmetz also found that parents often would record a series of events as one incident because the events were all related to the same causal event. The way in which parents chose to record conflicts eventually affected the total number of conflicts observed. Finally, parents were at times too busy to record their children's behavior. Recording the violent incidents at a later time increased the probability that some occurrences of sibling conflict could have been forgotten. Regardless of the shortcomings in the recording technique,

Steinmetz was able to demonstrate that sibling violence was occurring and the frequency of occurrences appeared to be quite high. In subsequent studies Steinmetz (1982) found that between 63% and 68% of adolescent siblings in the families she studied used physical violence to resolve conflicts with brothers and sisters.

Several years later, a team of sociologists (Straus, Gelles, & Steinmetz, 1980) conducted a nationally representative study on family violence. Sibling violence was one of several forms of family violence investigated. They reported the startling statistic that slightly more than four out of five (82%) children between the ages of 3 and 17, residing in the United States, and having one or more siblings living at home, engaged in at least one violent act toward a sibling during a one-year period. This translates into approximately 36.3 million children being violent toward a sibling within a year's time. Much of the violence that siblings engage in includes pushing, slapping, shoving, and throwing things. Some people have argued that these behaviors are not really serious and serve to overestimate the real rates of sibling violence. Therefore, when these "lesser" forms of violence are excluded and the researchers examine only the more severe forms of violence (such as kicking, biting, pushing, hitting with an object, and "beating up"), the rates are still alarmingly high. Straus and his colleagues estimate that over 19 million children a year engage in acts of abusive violence against a sibling.

Factors Related to Sibling Violence

Sex. Given that sibling violence occurs with alarming frequency, the question is raised as to whether all children engage in these violent acts with the same frequency or if these aggressive actions are being carried out by a particular category of children. While children of all ages and both sexes engage in violence and abuse against a brother or sister, there appears to be some difference in the rates at which they are violent. A commonly held belief in our society is that boys are more physically aggressive and girls are more verbally aggressive. One would expect then that sibling violence is initiated primarily by brothers. Although the research on sibling violence tends to support this commonsense belief, the support is not as overwhelming as one might expect (Straus, Gelles, & Steinmetz, 1980). While 83% of boys were aggressive toward a brother or sister, so were 74% of girls! At

TABLE 5.1 Incidence of Hidden Forms of Family Violence (in percentages)

Violent Acts	Sibling to Sibling	Parent to Adolescent	Adolescent to Parent
Any violence	82	46	9
Pushed or shoved	74	25	6
Slapped	48	28	3
Threw things	43	4	4
Kicked, bit, or punched	42	2	2
Hit, or tried to hit, with an object	40	7	2
Beaten up	16	1.3	0.7
Threatened with a knife or gun	0.8	0.2	0.3
Used a knife or gun	0.3	0.2	0.2

NOTE: This table is based on data collected by Straus, Gelles, and Steinmetz (1980).

all ages girls were less violent than boys, but the difference was relatively small.

Age. Research into sibling violence also confirms the belief that, as children grow older, the rates of using violence to resolve conflicts between siblings decrease (Steinmetz, 1977; Straus, Gelles, & Steinmetz, 1980). This could be the result of children becoming better equipped at using verbal skills to settle disputes. Also, as children grow older, they spend less and less time in each other's company. Older children spend more time away from home and away from potential sibling conflicts.

Steinmetz found that the factors precipitating conflicts varied with age. Younger children were more likely to have conflicts centered on possessions, especially toys. One family in Steinmetz's sample reported that, during a one-week period, their young children fought over "the use of a glider, sharing a truck, sharing a tricycle, knocking down one child's building blocks and taking them." Young adolescent conflicts focused on territory, with adolescents becoming very upset if a sibling invaded their personal space. "They fuss. They say, 'He's sitting in my seat,' or 'He has got an inch of his pants on the line where I am supposed to be' " (Steinmetz, 1977, p. 53). One father, driven to the breaking point by his children constantly fighting in the back seat of the car, took a can of red paint and painted boundary lines on the backseat and floor in an attempt to end disputes over personal space. Teenage conflicts, although less in number, still exist. These conflicts centered on responsibilities, obligations, and social awareness. Teenagers were more likely to be verbally aggressive and found that hollering was usually effective in conflict situations, especially when the siblings differed in opinions.

Other factors. Little is known about the factors that may be potentially associated with sibling violence. Those who have studied sibling murder often attribute the cause of such extreme aggression to jealousy. Dr. Adelson, after examining several children who had committed murder, concluded that preschoolers are capable of homicidal rage when they are threatened regarding their sense of security in the family unit. Kay Tooley's (1977) investigation of "murderously aggressive children" suggests that younger victims of sibling violence may sometimes be family scapegoats. However, it has not yet been established whether lesser forms of sibling aggression can be attributed to the same factors believed to be associated with murder.

Research on violent adolescents generally concludes that the factors associated with intimate adult violence (child abuse and spouse abuse) are of little use in helping to explain violence among children (Cornell & Gelles, 1982). In other words, children are not committing acts of violence for the same reasons as adults.

Finally, some researchers have postulated that sibling violence is a learned response. Although it is commonly believed that children will resort to violence as a natural way to resolve conflicts, the sociologists Straus, Gelles, and Steinmetz (1980) believe that siblings learn from their parents that physical punishment is an appropriate technique for resolving conflicts. Children raised in nonviolent environments learn that there are a variety of nonviolent techniques available for resolving conflicts with brothers and sisters and later with their spouses and children.

VIOLENCE TOWARD ADOLESCENTS

Although young children are the most frequent targets of physical abuse, abuse is *not* limited to very young children (see Chapter 3). Preteens and teenagers experience a wide range of violent treatments at the hands of their parents. While it is true that the rates of physical violence and abuse decline as children grow older, researchers who have examined the rates of adolescent victimization were surprised at the number of teenagers being mistreated in American families.

Societal attitudes perpetuate the myth that adolescents are rarely abused by their parents. As teenagers acquire greater physical strength with age, parents may begin to fear retaliation at the hands of children whose physical strength may surpass their own. For those children who are being struck, many people believe they precipitate or deserve being hit. Common sense sometimes suggests that teenagers frustrate their parents to such an extent that they deserve what they get!

The status of adolescents in our society is much the same as that of younger children. Both are considered the property and responsibility of their parents. Parents are granted societal permission to engage in a wide range of behaviors when disciplining their offspring. Although parents are expected to practice restraint when disciplining, the use of physical punishment is sanctioned as an acceptable behavior even for teenage children. Both young children and adolescents are relegated to a subordinate position within the family structure with parents being granted the right to bestow rewards and punishments as they see fit (Gil, 1970). Both preschoolers and teenagers are known for their difficult stages of development. Frustration in parents is often generated from young children going through the "terrible twos" stage. The "terrible twos" may be revisited as teenagers go through a stage of rebellion and independence. Preschool children are too young to be reasoned with, and teenagers do not wish to be reasoned with. It is this ability to generate frustration within their parents and create stress in the family unit as a whole that places young children and teenagers in the vulnerable position of being victimized. Adolescents reach a point in their development in which they are able to make effective use of the verbal skills they have acquired through years of conflict resolution with family members. The biggest complaint among parents of adolescents in Steinmetz's study on parent-child conflict was the "smart talk mouthiness" used by adolescents in both sibling and parent-child interactions. Steinmetz describes the adolescents in her sample as being "verbally aggressive" and frequently engaging in hollering, threatening, and arguing (Steinmetz, 1977).

If the position of young children and teenagers is so similar in our society, why has society become so deeply concerned with protecting the rights of younger children while ignoring the plight of adolescents? The answer to this question can again be traced to differences in expectations parents have for their younger children versus their older children. Parents expect their adolescents to begin acting in a more mature and responsible manner as they approach adulthood. They expect adolescents to be able to follow orders and to begin internalizing their system of values. Parents do not hold the same expectations for their preschoolers. Therefore, when adolescents fail to live up to their parents' expectations of them, parents sometimes use physical force as a way of asserting their parental control. Society is more likely to condone the use of physical force directed at an adolescent due to the belief that adolescents deserve such treatment.

Adolescents are also perceived as being better able to fend for themselves in disputes with their parents. Adolescents are larger, stronger, and, therefore, better able to protect themselves or avoid confrontations altogether. While this may be true, Mulligan (1977), in her sample of over 250 college students attending an eastern university, found that 8 in 100 students in her sample had been physically injured by a parent while they lived at home during their senior year of high school. Even though children between the ages of 5 and 14 are abused more frequently, children between the ages of 15 and 17 are more likely to have parents use "dangerous" forms of violence against them (Straus, Gelles, & Steinmetz, 1980). In this case, examination of simple frequency statistics fails to tell the entire story regarding the seriousness of teenage victimization.

Extent of Violence Toward Adolescents

Although researchers are not in total agreement as to the exact extent of adolescent abuse, they do agree that violence toward adolescents is a legitimate and significant form of family violence that occurs more frequently than is generally assumed. In fact, researchers have been generally surprised at the rate at which parents were physically abusing their adolescent and teenage children. The national survey of officially recognized and reported child maltreatment (Burgdorf, 1980) found that 47% of recognized victims of maltreatment were between the ages of 12 and 17. Data collected by the American Humane Association reveal that adolescents represented about 25% of officially reported victims of maltreatment for the years 1976-1979, 1981, and 1982 (Trainor, 1984). Other studies place the incidence somewhere between these two extremes (Garbarino & Carlson, 1979; Garbarino & Gilliam, 1980; Lourie, 1977, 1979; Olson & Holmes, 1986). Survey data from Straus and his colleagues' nationally representative study on family violence (1980) reveal that 54% of preteen and early teenage children (10 to 14 years of age) were struck by a parent while 33% of teens aged 15 to 17 were also hit during a one-year period (see Table 5.1). While younger children were more likely to be punched, grabbed, slapped, spanked, kicked, bitten, and hit with a fist or an object, teenage children were more likely to be "beaten up" and have a knife or gun used against them. Very young children (under 5) and teenagers were the most likely to experience violence that had a strong chance of inflicting physical injury. Adolescents stand a good chance of being physically injured, regardless of their increased size and physical strength. Mulligan (1977) found that 30% of the college students she sampled who were attending an eastern university were victimized by a parent at least once during their senior year of high school. Also, 8% of these teenagers were physically injured. The acts of violence against teenagers go beyond the "normal" forms of aggression used to discipline children.

Sex, Age, and Violence Toward Adolescents

Research findings depicting the relationship between sex and age of adolescents and the likelihood of violence and abuse are not always consistent. David Gil (1970), in his nationwide survey of child abuse, gathered information on abuse victims from cases reported through the central abuse registries in each state. Gil found only small differences between boys and girls at the younger ages, with boys being slightly more likely to be abused than girls. However, as children grow older, girls are more likely to be abused than boys. He attributed this finding to cultural attitudes regarding child-rearing practices in the United States. When children are younger, girls are more conforming than boys and require less discipline in the form of physical punishment. However, as children mature sexually, parents become more anxious over their daughters' heterosexual relationships. This anxiety leads to greater restrictions, increased conflict, and more frequent use of punishment to ensure parental control. With respect to boys, as they grow older, their physical strength increases and parents are less likely to use physical force because of fear of retaliation. Also, the same anxieties that exist concerning the sexual activities of daughters do not exist for sons. Similarly, the national survey of reported and recognized maltreatment found that girls are much more likely to be abused and neglected than are boys (Burgdorf, 1980).

Other researchers have found the relationship between sex and age of adolescents and likelihood of abuse to be the exact opposite as that found by Gil (Mulligan, 1977; Straus, Gelles, & Steinmetz, 1980). They found that young boys and girls were pushed, grabbed, shoved, slapped, and spanked at pretty much the same rate. But, as they grew older, boys over the age of 10 were more likely to experience these forms of behavior than girls. Boys 15 to 17 were twice as likely as girls to be pushed, grabbed, or shoved. Mulligan (1977) reports that the higher rates of violence toward boys can be partially explained in terms of "linkage theory" (Straus, 1971), which states that parents socialize their children in accordance with the type of personality skills they feel their children will need later in life. If parents anticipate that their sons will be faced with aggressive situations more often than their daughters, parents will be more likely to use physical force toward their sons. More recently, an analysis of data from the Second National Family Violence Survey (Wauchope & Straus, 1990) found no significant differences between adolescent boys and girls in terms of experiencing all forms of physical punishment.

How can we explain differences in the research findings concerning the age and sex of adolescents and their likelihood of abuse? Perhaps the answer lies in the techniques used by the researchers in collecting their information on abuse. Gil relied upon child abuse cases reported to public officials in the 50 states. Similarly, the national survey of reported and recognized maltreatment is based on public perceptions and recognition of maltreatment. Straus, Gelles, Steinmetz, and Mulligan relied upon self-reports of abuse. As has already been discussed in this book, the utilization of publicly identified cases of abuse has inherent problems. Perhaps girls were over-represented in Gil's study because cases of abuse involving females were more likely to be reported to public officials than cases involving boys. Boys are taught: "be tough" and "don't cry," and thus may be more likely to conceal their inflicted injuries than girls.

The difference in findings may also be due to differences in the definition of abuse. Straus, Gelles, Steinmetz, and Mulligan focused on violence without concern for whether an injury took place. Gil's definition of abuse was restricted to cases that produced an injury. Gil also studied many more forms of abusive violence (e.g., burning) than Straus and his colleagues or Mulligan. Perhaps females were more likely to be victims of the types of abuse not included in Straus and his colleagues' definition of victimization (such as strangling, drowning, burning, poisoning, or tying up or locking in).

Explaining Violence Toward Adolescents

Why are parents violent toward their adolescents and teenage children? One explanation is that they are violent and abusive toward their older children for the same reasons they are violent and abusive toward their younger children. In some instances, abuse of adolescents is an extension of violence that began when the teenager was a younger child. A second explanation is provided by Ira Lourie (1977), who points out that, as children grow physically stronger and seek independence, parents may resort to more violent means of control. Another possible factor might be the struggle for independence between adolescents and their parents. Adolescence is also a stressful period for children and parents. Finally, parents see in their adolescent offspring the consequences of their parenting and may feel upset or guilty about their parent roles. Obviously, we need much more research on this issue in order to draw any kind of informed conclusion.

PARENT ABUSE

The idea of children attacking their parents is so foreign to our conceptions of parent-child relations that it is difficult for most of us to believe that such behavior occurs. Parents are granted the position of authority and power in the family's status hierarchy. Parents command control of the family's resources, such as money, power, status, and violence. According to the sociologist William Goode, violence *is* a legitimate resource at the disposal of family members, and it will be used whenever other attempts at alleviating a conflict fail. It is logically assumed, however, that the use of violence to resolve conflicts is brought into play by the typically dominant member of the family to ensure submission of those in their care. Goode argues that wives and children could, and sometimes do, use force but it does not occur frequently due to greater normative disapproval of children and wives using force against the father or husband.

> The rebellious child or wife knows the father or husband is stronger, and can call upon outsiders who will support that force with more force. . . . The force or threat they command is not only their own strength but that of the community, which will back up the traditional family patterns. (Goode, 1971, pp. 625-626)

Societal attitudes concerning who uses violence within the family partially explain why this form of violence has been one of the least researched and, consequently, why, until recently, not very much is known about its extent, patterns, and causes.

Goode's quote alludes to other social attitudes that hinder recognition of parent abuse as a hidden form of family violence. Not only do children lack control of the family's resources, they are thought of as smaller and having less physical strength. This observation alone is enough to make us think that children are not physically capable of injuring their parents. However, what research is available graphically demonstrates that children can and do inflict injury upon their parents. For example, one clinical study reports on the case of an 11-year-old boy who became aggressive toward his mother after she spanked him for disobeying orders. He reportedly pushed her down, broke her coccyx, and then proceeded to kick her in the face while she was on the floor (Harbin & Madden, 1979). Carol Warren (1978), in her investigation of 15 battering adolescents between the ages of 12 and 17 who were admitted to a psychiatric hospital, found that what these children lacked in physical strength they more than made up for with speed and weapons. One 12-year-old "poured gasoline in the bathroom while his mother was in there, threw a match, and shut the door." These examples demonstrate that physical size and strength are not always the best indicator of who will be violent in a family.

Goode (1971) also quite accurately states that there is greater normative disapproval of children using violence against a parent than of a parent using violence against their children. The community supports parental rights and obligations while imposing strong sanctions against children who violate traditional family patterns concerning the legitimate use of force. Children's abuse of their parents is so counternormative that it is extremely difficult for parents to admit that they are being victimized by one of their children. Unless the children commit lethal acts or acts of extreme violence, it is rare that the behavior of violent children and adolescents comes to the public's attention. Discussion and reporting of such acts is almost a taboo subject because many parents are ashamed of their own victimization. Parents are afraid that others will blame them for their children's violent behavior. Parents of abusive children are believed to suffer from tremendous anxiety, depression, and guilt.

Henry Harbin and Dennis Madden (1979) examined 15 families identified as having an adolescent between the ages of 14 and 20 who was assaulting a parent. All these families were trying desperately to maintain an illusion of family harmony. Parents would occasionally admit to being abused by their children immediately following a particularly aggressive episode, but the "veil of denial" would rapidly reappear. Parents would try endlessly to protect their abusive offspring. Harbin and Madden identified four ways in which the veil of denial and protection manifested itself: (a) the families would try to avoid all discussion of the violent episodes; (b) all the family members would attempt to minimize the seriousness of the aggressive behavior; (c) the parents would avoid punishment for the abusive behavior; and (d) the families refused to ask for outside help either for themselves or for their child. The role of denial and the creation of an image of a peaceful and loving family plays an important part in abusive families. This role allows the family to continue functioning even though the family must continually deny the reality of violence (Ferreira, 1963). Admission of violent behavior on the part of the offspring or the parent may introduce the threat of family separation. The denial of reality serves as a defense mechanism to protect the family from outside observers and influence.

Extent of Violence Toward Parents

The investigations of violence toward parents that have been conducted all report the same result: The rate of child-to-parent violence, while being less than parent-to-child abuse, is large enough to warrant attention. The U.S. Department of Justice (1980) estimated that of the 1.2 million incidents of violence between relatives, 47,000 involved children's violence against parents. Most researchers find that the rates at which children abuse their parents range from 5% to 12%. Martha Mulligan (1977) reports that 12% of the college students she questioned used at least one form of violence against a parent while they lived at home during their senior year of high school. Charles Peek and his colleagues (1985) analyzed data collected from more than 1,500 parents of White male high school sophomores, juniors, and seniors as part of the Youth in Transition Survey. They found that between 7% and 11% of the parents reported being hit. Straus, Gelles, and Steinmetz (1980) found that 10% of the children 3 to 17 years of age in their sample performed at least one act of violence against a parent during a one-year period (see Table 5.1). Our own statistics (Cornell & Gelles, 1982), generated from a nationally representative sample of families who had a teenager living at home between the ages of 10 and 17, agreed with the findings of the other studies—9% of parents reported at least one act of violence. This translates into approximately 2.5 million parents being struck at least once a year. A statistic was also calculated for the more severe forms of violence. Approximately 3% of the adolescents were reported to have kicked, punched, bit, "beat up," or used a knife or gun against a parent. While this percentage appears quite small, when it is projected to the total number of adolescents between 10 and 17 living in two-parent households, it means that 900,000 parents are being abused each year. Robert Agnew and Sandra Huguley (1989) analyzed data from the 1972 National Survey of Youth and report that roughly 5% of the adolescents in the survey had hit one of their parents in the previous year.

Factors Related to Violence Toward Parents

Who is violent? Harbin and Madden (1979) found that the majority of children who attack a parent are between the ages of 13 and 24, although they also report on children as young as 10 years old inflicting injury on their parents. Researchers agree that sons are slightly more likely to be violent and abusive than daughters. The sons' rates of severe violence against a parent increase with age, while for daughters the rates of severe violence decline with age. Agnew and Huguley (1989) found that, as boys grew older, they were somewhat less likely to hit their mothers and more likely to hit their fathers. This suggests, perhaps, that boys do take advantage of increased size and strength that comes with adolescent growth. A social explanation could be that the boys and girls are adhering to the cultural norms that reward aggressiveness in teenage boys but negatively sanction the use of violence among teenage girls.

Researchers disagree as to whether mothers are more likely to be hit than fathers. Some studies support the belief that mothers are the most likely targets of children's aggression (Cornell & Gelles, 1982), while other data (U.S. Department of Justice, 1980) find fathers the more likely victims. An examination of police reports of formal complaints about adolescent aggression toward parents found that the modal pattern was male adolescent violence toward mothers (Evans & Warren-Sohlberg, 1988). The most recent examination of this issue concludes that mothers are more likely to be victims of their children's violence but that fathers are the more likely victims of older male children (Agnew & Huguley, 1989).

Clinical observations of adolescents who had abused a parent found that most families had some disturbance in the authority structure within the family. Adolescents had been granted too much control. Abused parents seemed to be turning to young or immature children for decision making. This tremendous responsibility on the shoulders of young people seemed to generate extreme frustration. Harbin and Madden (1979) claim that the physical attacks on the parent were often an attempt by the adolescents either to control the family or to punish the parents for placing them in the decision-making role in the first place. Many of the abusive children had very poor self-concepts; whenever they were challenged or made to feel insecure, anxiety was created, often resulting in violent episodes.

While child abuse and spouse abuse have been found to be related to many social, family structural, and situational factors, adolescent violence does not seem to vary in any meaningful way with these same factors. Adolescent violence cannot be explained using the same social factors that explain adult violence. The data do appear to indicate, though, that the rates of parent abuse are related to the frequency of other forms of family violence in the home. The more violence children experience or witness, the more likely they are to strike out at a parent. These findings are consistent with the theory that families who view violence as a legitimate way to resolve conflict run a greater risk of experiencing all forms of family violence, including parent abuse. Adolescents who have friends who assault parents, who approve of delinquency under certain conditions, who perceive the possibility of being arrested as low, and who are weakly attached to their parents have been found to be the most likely to use violence toward their parents (Agnew & Huguley, 1989).

ELDER ABUSE

Abuse of the elderly is the only form of "hidden" family violence that has managed to generate a significant amount of public concern. This concern is, however, a very recent development. Prior to the 1980s, elder abuse received about as much social recognition as parent abuse, adolescent abuse, and sibling violence. There are several easily identifiable factors that can help explain society's recent interest in this topic. Major demographic changes that have occurred over the last half century have increased the number of older Americans in our population. This is a direct result of the life expectancy of the average person increasing by nearly 50% in approximately 50 years (U.S. Bureau of the Census, 1978). As elderly people live longer and the fertility rate declines, the proportion of the elderly people in the population also increases. This growing number of older Americans has heightened our awareness of the many problems being experienced by the elderly. These changes have, in turn, had an impact upon family responsibilities. As people live longer, there is a growing need for middle-aged children to share the responsibility for caring for an aged parent. Of those between 65 and 72 years of age, only one elderly person in fifty needs long-term care. But, among those 73 years of age and over, the chances increase to one in fifteen (Koch & Koch, 1980). Children having responsibility for caring for their aging parents is also a relatively new and growing aspect of family life. For these reasons, researchers have become interested in studying the consequences of caring for aging parents in the home. They realize that it is impractical to expect all families to have the appropriate financial, emotional, and social resources to handle this additional burden.

The recognition of elder abuse as a social problem and the subsequent identification of abuse victims has not been an easy task. Many obstacles have stood in the way. To begin with, the elderly are not tied into many social networks, such as mandatory schooling or employment, that facilitate easier identification of victims. The elderly are, on average, even more isolated from the mainstream of society than younger adults. This isolation allows violent behavior to continue unimpeded, with elderly victims confined to their homes, often dependent upon those who are abusing them. Identification of abuse victims is also hindered by the elderly victims' unwillingness to report incidents of maltreatment to the authorities. Only one in four known cases of abuse are reported by the victims themselves (Legal Research and Services for the Elderly, 1979). No one knows how many cases exist that go unreported! Sometimes friends, relatives, or neighbors are aware of what is happening but they are frightened and unsure of what to do. In the majority of cases, however, elder abuse becomes known to the authorities through a third party (Legal Research and Services for the Elderly, 1979). Even after the occurrence of abuse has been reported and substantiated, many abuse victims are unwilling to admit to it.

There are a number of reasons to explain their hesitancy. Due to societal attitudes, many elderly family members are too embarrassed to admit that they have raised a child capable of such behavior. Again, as with other forms of family violence, they assume the blame for the abuser's behavior. Frequently, their love for the abuser is stronger than the desire to leave the abusive situation. They are more concerned for the welfare of the abuser than for their own safety and well-being. They are unwilling to begin any legal action that might result in some sort of punishment for the abuser and, consequently, further their own isolation. This fear of isolation is a result of the majority of victims living in the same house as their abuser (Legal Research and Services for the Elderly, 1979). If elderly people are physically, emotionally, or economically dependent upon their abusers, they may be unsure of what alternatives are available to them if they do report the abuse. An important problem is that the alternatives available to aged family members who may wish to leave an abusive environment are often considered worse than the abusive situation. In particular, the elderly victim often considers institutionalized care as the worst possible alternative. This fear of institutionalization is apparently a valid one. Lau and Kosberg (1979), in their study of abuse victims reported to the Cleveland Chronic Illness Center, report that 46% of the cases of elder abuse eventually resulted in institutionalization of the victim. In 26% of the cases, assistance was refused by the victim, and in 28% of the cases, assistance other than institutionalization was offered and accepted.

Another factor that hinders identification of abuse victims is the low level of awareness among public service agencies regarding the issue of elderly abuse. Agencies dealing with the elderly were initially very reluctant to become involved in abuse cases. They were concerned about violations of confidentiality. When the issue of confidentiality had been resolved, the agencies often did not have the personnel and resources available to effectively handle reported cases. It has been noted that these were precisely the same issues that hindered action in the identification, awareness, and treatment of child abuse 20 years earlier (Rathbone-McCuan, 1980).

Nature and Extent of Elder Abuse

Abusive treatment toward the elderly can take many forms. Caretakers may tie an aged relative to a bed or chair while they go out shopping or finish their housework. They may overmedicate their parents to "ease" the older person's discomfort and to make them more manageable. Other caretakers resort to physical attacks to "make them mind" or to coerce their elderly relatives into changing a will or signing the house or social security checks over to them. Some caretakers may have used such excessive physical violence or have neglected the needs of the older persons to such an extent that death has resulted.

It is difficult to assess exactly how many elderly people are abused each year. While several state agencies have tried to measure the extent of abuse in their individual states, resources have not been allocated to conduct a nationally representative study. Estimates of the proportion of those 65 years of age or older range from 4% to 10% (Pagelow, 1989). The frequency of elder abuse could vary from 500,000 cases a year (for acts of physical violence alone) to 2.5 million cases annually (U.S. Congress, 1980). Karl Pillemer and David Finkelhor (1988) conducted the first large-scale random sample survey of elder abuse and neglect. Interviews were conducted with 2,020 community dwelling (noninstitutionalized) elderly persons in the Boston metropolitan area. Overall, 32 elderly persons per 1,000 reported experiencing physical violence, verbal aggression, and/or neglect in the past year. The rate of physical violence was 20 per 1,000. Although the conventional view of elder abuse is that of middle-aged children abusing and neglecting the elderly parents, Pillemer and Finkelhor found that spouses were the most frequent abusers of the elderly and that roughly equal numbers of men and women were victims. Women, however, suffered from the most serious forms of abuse. The rate of child-to-parent abuse was between 20 and 80 per 1,000, with daughter-to-father being the rarest form of abuse and son-to-mother or father being the most common form. The rate of physical violence ranged from 10 to 40 per 1,000.

The larger estimates of elder abuse have resulted from defining "abuse" as physical, emotional, psychological, and self-abuse, in addition to passive and active neglect. The development of an adequate and acceptable definition of elder abuse has been, perhaps, the most significant impediment in developing an adequate knowledge base on elder abuse. The variety of definitions in the current studies makes the task of comparing the results of the research nearly impossible. Naturally, the broader one's definition of abuse, the greater the number of incidents per year.

Factors Related to Elder Abuse

Based upon the existing data, the most likely victim of elder abuse is a female of very advanced age (Senstock & Liang, 1983). One of the most commonly cited causal factors in the elder abuse literature is the resentment generated by the dependency of an older person on a caretaker. Research reports that victims of elder abuse often suffer from physical and/or mental impairments and are dependent upon their caretakers for many, if not most, of their daily needs (Block & Sinnott, 1979; Legal Research and Services for the Elderly, 1979; Rathbone-McCuan, 1980; Schaie, 1982; Steinmetz, 1978c). It is this dependent situation of the elderly that increases their likelihood of being abused. Suzanne Steinmetz (1978c) notes that several parallels exist between child abuse and elder abuse. Both children and the elderly are in dependent positions in the family and rely upon their caregivers for the provision of basic needs. Both are presumed to be protected and adequately cared for within the family setting, and both can become a source of economic, physical, or emotional strain. Steinmetz believes that, while most couples expect to care for children, they do not always anticipate the possibility of caring for their aged parents. The process of caring for elderly parents presents unique problems for any family. While children become less and less dependent with age, the health of aging relatives renders them more and more dependent.

New research reports the finding that abusers are financially dependent on their victims (Hawalek, Senstock, & Lawrence, 1984; Pillemer, 1985; Wolf, Strugnell, & Godkin, 1982). The explanation for this contradiction to the commonsense explanation for the occurrence of elder abuse is that abuse is an act carried out as a response to perceived powerlessness (Finkelhor, 1983). The adult child who is still dependent on the elderly parent may strike out or maltreat as a compensation for their lack, or loss, of power. Dependency appears to play a crucial role in abuse of the elderly, but it is not yet clear who is dependent on whom (Pillemer & Suiter, 1988).

Initial research reported that the abuser is typically identified as being female, middle-aged, and usually the offspring of the abused. More recent research suggests that males are slightly more likely to be abusers (Pillemer, 1985; Senstock & Liang, 1983). There has yet to be a systematic exploration of the relationship between stress and elder abuse, although some exploratory research indicates that stress may be related to elder abuse (Senstock & Liang, 1983).

Some researchers find that victims of elder abuse were at one time abusive toward their children; however, there is no systematic evidence that the intergenerational transmission of violence is strongly related to elder abuse (Pillemer & Suiter, 1988). Elder abuse may be an extension of the child abuse syndrome. The adult children learned, through personal experience or observation, that the use of violence was an acceptable response to a stressful situation. The violent resolution of stressful situations runs in the family and is passed on from generation to generation.

SUMMARY

It is quite clear that the rates of the "hidden" forms of private violence are as high or higher than the better-known types of violence. Our understanding of the hidden victims of violence is limited because there has been very little research on these forms of violence. The data on sibling violence and violence toward parents are either anecdotal or come from Straus and his colleagues' National Family Violence Survey (1980). Even in that survey, sibling violence and violence toward parents was added as almost an afterthought, and the survey failed to ask many questions specific to these types of violence. Data on elder abuse are limited and, when available, typically come from small samples or case studies. Similarly, data on violence toward adolescents come either from small case studies or from parts of the National Family Violence Survey.

One hopes that, as we gain a better understanding of violence in the home, we will recognize that it is certainly not directed solely toward young children and women. A perspective that recognizes that all family relationships can be and sometimes are violent might help us to broaden our examination into the generative sources of intimate violence. The next chapter attempts to apply that broader perspective and present a general theory of family violence.

DISCUSSION QUESTIONS

(1) Why have the "hidden forms" of family violence been overlooked? How does blaming the victim contribute to keeping certain forms of family violence hidden? How do cultural norms and values concerning children, parents, and the elderly contribute to keeping certain forms of family violence hidden?
(2) Why has elderly abuse received more attention than the other forms of hidden violence?
(3) What are some of the factors related to hidden forms of violence? How do the factors related to hidden violence compare with factors related to the abuse of young children or violence between spouses?

SUGGESTED ASSIGNMENTS

(1) Find out if your state has mandatory reporting laws for cases of elder abuse. Who is required to report? How many cases are reported each year? Has there been an increase in reporting in the last few years? What services are available in your community, city, or state for victims of elder abuse?
(2) Conduct a survey and measure people's awareness of and attitudes toward the known forms of family violence (child abuse or wife abuse) and the hidden forms. Be sure to ask parallel questions so that you can compare the results.

CHAPTER
6

Explaining Family Violence

THE DISCUSSION IN previous chapters about the factors that are related to various types of family violence shed some light on our understanding of why parents batter children, husbands abuse wives, and other family members assault their siblings and parents. Nevertheless, a list of factors associated with family violence still does not complete our understanding. People with low incomes may be more likely to abuse a family member, but income is *not a complete explanation* of family violence.

This chapter first examines profiles of child and wife batterers in order to get a composite picture of how the various factors combine to produce violence. The following section poses the question: Why is the family such a violent institution? The answer can be found by looking at some of the unique characteristics of the family as a social group. Finally, we review some of the models that have been used to explain family violence, and we conclude with an integrated social exchange/social control explanation.

PROFILES OF VIOLENT HOMES

One way of advancing our understanding of family violence is to move beyond a simple examination of single factors and their association with violence. After considering all the variables that are found to be related with violence in the home, Straus and his colleagues added the factors together to get a profile of child abusers and spouse abusers.

A Profile of Child Abuse

Although it is really impossible to characterize the "typical" child abuser, there are a number of characteristics of individuals and families that, when combined, increase the chances that abuse will occur.

Homes with the greatest risk of child abuse are homes character-
ized by Straus, Gelles, and Steinmetz (1980) as having

(1) both parents being verbally aggressive with the children;
(2) more than the average amount of conflict between the husband and
wife;
(3) the husband being verbally aggressive toward his wife;
(4) the husband being aggressive toward his wife;
(5) the husband being a manual worker;
(6) the husband being dissatisfied with his standard of living;
(7) the wife being a manual worker or a full-time housekeeper;
(8) the wife being less than 30 years old;
(9) the wife and the husband having been physically punished as children;
(10) two or more children in the home;
(11) the couple having been married less than 10 years;
(12) having lived in their neighborhood less than two years;
(13) the father participating in no organized community groups; or
(14) the father growing up in a family where his mother hit his father.

Families that failed to include any one of the above characteristics
reported *no* abusive violence toward children. Families where all 14
factors were present had a three in ten chance of using abusive
violence toward their children. Obviously, this is not a perfect explanation for the presence or absence of child abuse, but it does give some
insight into what kinds of situations increase the risk of abuse for
children.

A Profile of Wife Abuse

Straus and associates (1980) found 20 characteristics relevant in acts
of wife beating. They include the following:

(1) the husband employed part-time or unemployed;
(2) family income under $6,000;
(3) the husband a manual worker (if employed);
(4) both husband and wife very worried about economic security;
(5) the wife dissatisfied with the family's standard of living;
(6) two or more children;
(7) frequent disagreements over children;
(8) husband and wife having grown up in families where the father hit
the mother;
(9) couples married less than ten years;

(10) the husband and wife both less than 30 years of age;
(11) couples who are members of a non-White racial group;
(12) above-average marital conflict;
(13) very high levels of family and individual stress;
(14) the wife or husband dominating family decisions;
(15) a husband verbally aggressive to his wife;
(16) a wife verbally aggressive to her husband;
(17) both getting drunk frequently, but are not alcoholics;
(18) couples who lived in a neighborhood less than two years;
(19) couples who do not participate in organized religion; or
(20) the wife a full-time housewife.

Again, as with the profile of child abusive families, if none of these characteristics was present, there was no reported spouse abuse in the home. Those families that were unfortunate enough to have more than 12 of the factors had better than a six in ten chance of some reported wife abuse in the previous year.

It might be tempting to think that we could use these profiles to predict where and when family abuse will occur. Unfortunately, this would generate many more problems than it would solve. Because the profiles are not 100% accurate (for example, 70% of the homes with all the child abuse risk factors still do not abuse their children; three in ten families with all the wife abuse characteristics do not have wife abuse), we would run the very dangerous risk of falsely predicting many people as child or wife beaters. The negative consequences of false labeling would certainly cancel out the good that would be derived from being able to predict, in advance, some families who will become abusive.

VIOLENCE AND THE
ORGANIZATION OF FAMILY LIFE

For much of this book we have concentrated on examining the characteristics of individuals and family relations and how these characteristics are related to various types of family violence. To concentrate only on individuals and family relations would, to a certain extent, miss the forest for the trees. While many people consider the most important question in the study of family violence to be this: "Who are the abusive family members and why are they abusive?" There is another equally important question: "Why are families so violent?" Once we have completed our examination of the incidence and extent of the various types of family violence, we are left with the quite inescapable conclusion that the family is society's most violent institution, excepting only the military in times of war. Why is the family the place where one is most likely to be killed, physically assaulted, hit, beaten up, slapped, or spanked? Why is violence perhaps as common as love in families? Until we consider the social organization of the family that makes it violence prone, we have not adequately addressed the questions with which we opened this book.

Richard Gelles and Murray Straus (1979) identified the unique characteristics of the family as a social group that contribute to making the family a violence-prone institution. Later, Straus, with his colleague Gerald Hotaling (1979), noted the irony that these same characteristics we saw as making the family violence prone also serve to make the family a warm, supportive, and intimate environment. Briefly, these factors are as follows:

(1) *Time at risk.* The ratio of time spent interacting with family members far exceeds the ratio of time spent interacting with others, although the ratio will vary depending on stages in the family life cycle.

(2) *Range of activities and interests.* Not only do family members spend a great deal of time with one another, the interaction ranges over a much wider spectrum of activities than nonfamilial interaction.

(3) *Intensity of involvement.* The quality of family interaction is also unique. The degree of commitment to family interaction is greater. A cutting remark made by a family member is likely to have a much larger impact than the same remark in another setting.

(4) *Impinging activities.* Many interactions in the family are inherently conflict-structured and have a "zero sum" aspect. Whether it involves deciding which television show to watch or what car to buy, there will be both winners and losers in family relations.

(5) *Right to influence.* Belonging to a family carries with it the implicit right to influence the values, attitudes, and behaviors of other family members.

(6) *Age and sex differences.* The family is unique in that it is made up of different ages and sexes. Thus there is the potential for a battle between generations *and* sexes.

(7) *Ascribed roles.* In addition to the problem of age and sex differences there is the fact that the family is perhaps the only social institution that assigns roles and responsibilities based on age and sex rather than interest or competence.

(8) *Privacy.* The modern family is a private institution, insulated from the eyes, ears, and often rules of the wider society. Where privacy is high, the degree of social control will be low.

(9) *Involuntary membership.* Families are exclusive organizations. Birth relationships are involuntary and cannot be terminated. While there can be ex-wives and ex-husbands, there are no ex-children or ex-parents. Being in a family involves personal, social, material, and legal commitment and entrapment. When conflict arises it is not easy to break off the conflict by fleeing the scene or resigning from the group.

(10) *Stress.* Families are prone to stress. This is due in part to the theoretical notion that dyadic relationships are unstable (Simmel, 1950). Moreover, families are constantly undergoing changes and transitions. The birth of children, maturation of children, aging, retirement, and death are all changes recognized by family scholars. Moreover, stress felt by one family member (such as unemployment, illness, bad grades at school) is transmitted to other family members.

(11) *Extensive knowledge of social biographies.* The intimacy and emotional involvement of family relations reveal a full range of identities to members of a family. Strengths and vulnerabilities, likes and dislikes, loves and fears are all known to family members. While this knowledge can help support a relationship, the information can also be used to attack intimates and can lead to conflict.

It is one thing to say that the social organization of the family makes it a conflict-prone institution and social group. However, the 11 characteristics we listed do not supply the complete answer. The key additional consideration is one we discussed in Chapter 2. The fact that the social organization of the family we have just described exists within a cultural context where violence is tolerated, accepted, and even mandated is a critical factor that helps us understand why the family, as currently structured, can be loving, supportive, *and* violent. The widespread acceptability of physical punishment in raising children creates a situation where a conflict-prone institution serves as a training ground to teach children that it is acceptable (a) to hit people you love, (b) for powerful people to hit less powerful people, (c) to use hitting to achieve some end or goal, and (d) to hit as an end in itself.

MODELS THAT EXPLAIN FAMILY VIOLENCE

The Psychiatric Model

Although we have discussed the psychiatric model previously and have found that this explanation for family violence is too limited, its popularity in the professional literature as well as among the general public causes us to repeat a description of the model and its problems one more time.

The tragic picture of a defenseless child, woman, or grandparent subjected to abuse and neglect arouses the strongest emotions in clinicians and others who see and/or treat the problem of intimate violence. There frequently seems to be no rational explanation for harming a loved one. It is not surprising, therefore, that a psychiatric model of family violence was the first applied to the problem and that it has endured for years, even in the absence of strong scientific evidence to support it. Even sociologists can find themselves using such a model. One of us (Gelles) once was working in a clinic at Children's Hospital of Boston. We were examining and doing a psycho-social-medical evaluation of a young child who had suffered a severe immersion burn (she had been forced into a bathtub filled with scalding hot water). It was obvious that she had been purposely burned, because she had been pressed against the tub with such force that neither the soles of her feet or her bottom had been burned. After the scalding, she had apparently been tied to the bed and this had resulted in lacerations of her wrists and ankles. After our examination, we returned to our offices and wrote up our clinic notes. Our colleague, Eli Newberger (he is referenced at times in this text), came by and asked us what we thought about the case. We responded, "Anyone who would do that is crazy!" Eli looked puzzled. "Aren't you the person who wrote in 1973 that the psychopathological model of abuse was a myth?" he asked Gelles. (I did, and my model is presented in Chapter 3, RJG.) "I don't care what I wrote," Gelles responded, "I know what I saw!"

The psychiatric model focuses on the abuser's personality characteristics as the chief determinants of violence and abuse. A psychiatric model links factors such as mental illness, personality defects, psychopathology, sociopathology, alcohol and drug misuse, or other intraindividual abnormalities to family violence. Research indicates that fewer than 10% of instances of family violence are attributable solely to personality traits, mental illness, or psychopathology (Steele, 1978; Straus, 1980).

In closing this discussion, it is important to speculate why, despite the lack of scientific evidence, people (including us, at times) persist in applying the psychiatric model to more cases of family violence than is warranted. The answer may lie, paradoxically, in the fact that family violence is so extensive in our society that we do not want to recognize it as a pattern of family relations. Somehow, we do not want to consider our own potential to abuse or even consider that some of the acts we engage in (pushing a wife, slapping a child) are violent or abusive. If we can persist in believing that violence and abuse are the products of aberrations or sickness, and, therefore, believe ourselves to be well, then our acts cannot be hurtful or abusive. Furthermore, the psychiatric model serves as an ideal smokescreen to blind us from considering social organizational factors that cause family violence.

A Social-Situational Model

That personality problems and psychopathology do not fully explain acts of family violence does not mean that personal problems are unrelated to intimate abuse. These personal problems, however, tend to arise from social antecedents. We have reviewed those social factors, such as conflict, unemployment, isolation, unwanted pregnancy, and stress, in previous chapters.

A social-situational model of family violence proposes that abuse and violence arise out of two main factors. The first is structural stress. The association between low income and family violence, for instance, indicates that a central factor in violence and abuse is inadequate financial resources. The second main factor is the cultural norm concerning force and violence in the home (see Chapter 2). "Spare the rod and spoil the child." "The marriage license is a hitting license." These are phrases that underscore the widespread social approval for the use of force and violence at home.

The social-situational model notes that such structural stresses as low income, unemployment, limited educational resources, illness, and the like are unevenly distributed in society. While all groups are told that they should be loving parents, adoring husbands, and caring wives, only some groups get sufficient resources to meet these demands. Others fall considerably short of being able to have the psychological, social, and economic resources to meet the expectations of society, friends, neighbors, loved ones, and themselves. Combined with the cultural approval for violence, these shortfalls lead many family members to adopt violence and abuse as a means of coping with structural stress.

Social Learning Theory

A subset of social-situational theory is social learning theory. A commonly stated explanation for family violence is that people learn to be violent when they grow up in violent homes. The family is the first place where people learn the roles of mother and father, husband and wife. The family is one key place where we learn how to cope with stress and frustration. The family is also the place where people are most likely to first experience violence. We have already seen in previous chapters that violence is frequently transmitted from generation to generation. Again, we must warn that not all victims of violence grow up to be violent themselves. But a history of abuse and violence does increase the risk that an individual will be violent as an adult.

Individuals are not only exposed to techniques of being violent, they also learn the social and moral justifications for the behavior. It is not uncommon to hear a parent who has struck his or her own child explain that they were punishing the child for the child's own good. We have interviewed many parents who use exactly the same physical punishment on their children that they themselves experienced (some even use the exact same objects, which must have been passed down from generation to generation).

Resource Theory

Another explanation of family violence that is supported by the available scientific data is resource theory (Goode, 1971). This model assumes that all social systems (including the family) rest to some degree on force or the threat of force. The more resources—social, personal, and economic—a person can command, the more force he or she can muster. However, according to William Goode, the author of this theory, the more resources a person actually has, the less he or she will actually use force in an open manner. Thus a husband who wants to be the dominant person in the family but has little education, has a job low in prestige and income, and lacks interpersonal skills may choose to use violence to maintain the dominant position. In addition, family members (including children) may use violence to redress a grievance when they have few alternative resources available.

An Ecological Perspective

The psychologist James Garbarino (1977) has proposed an "ecological model" to explain the complex nature of child maltreatment. Garbarino applies what he refers to as the ecological, or human development, approach. This model concentrates on the progressive, mutual adaptation of the organism (in this case, family members) and the environment. Garbarino concerns himself not just with the family but with the complex interrelation of the many social systems that overlap with family life and influence human development. A major concern of Garbarino is "social habitability," or the quality of the environment in which the person and family develop. Garbarino also considers the political, economic, and social factors that shape the quality of life for children and their families.

From these complex series of overlapping factors and influences, Garbarino extracts two key elements that help explain the existence of child abuse. The first, as has been stated so often, is cultural support for using physical force against children. The second is the level of family support in the environment. The less family support (one factor might be fewer available day-care centers), the greater the risk of maltreatment of children.

In short, the ecological model proposes that violence and abuse arise out of a mismatch of parent to child and family to neighborhood and community. To somewhat oversimplify, the risk of abuse and violence is greatest when the functioning of the children and parents is limited and constrained by developmental problems. Children with learning disabilities or social or emotional handicaps are at increased risk for abuse. Parents under considerable stress or who have personality problems are at increased risk for abusing their children. These conditions are worsened when social interaction between the spouses or the parents and children heighten the stress or make the personal problems worse. Finally, if there are few institutions and agencies in the community to support troubled families, then the risk of abuse is further raised.

Garbarino has found that the highest rates of child abuse are found in communities that have the fewest human and social service agencies. Rates are high in homes where marital conflict and stress are the highest and among families who are socially isolated. Last, specific personal and social characteristics of children and parents increase the likelihood for abuse.

Patriarchy and Wife Abuse

The previous models of family violence have been different only in degree. They tend to examine individuals and family relations in their search for the explanation for family violence. The final model we examine is quite different. The sociologists Russell and Rebecca Dobash (1979) see wife abuse as a unique phenomenon that has been obscured and overshadowed by what they refer to as the "narrow" focus on domestic violence. As we noted earlier in this book, the Dobashes make the case that, throughout history, violence has systematically been directed toward women. The Dobashes' central thesis is that economic and social processes operate directly and indirectly to support a patriarchal (male-dominated) social order and family structure. Their central theoretical argument is that patriarchy leads to the subordination of women and causes the historical pattern of systematic violence directed against wives.

The Dobashes' theory is perhaps the only theory that finds the source of family violence in the society and how it is organized, as opposed to within individual families or communities. The major drawback of the theory is that it uses but a single factor (patriarchy) to explain violence, and single-factor explanations are rarely useful in social science.

AN EXCHANGE/SOCIAL CONTROL THEORY OF FAMILY VIOLENCE

Some time ago we were called by a newspaper reporter who was writing an editorial on family violence. He wanted us to give him a short one- or two-sentence statement on why family members use violence on one another. At first, the thought of boiling down many years of research into some kind of quotable-quote seemed impossible. But we had been wrestling for some time with a project that was aimed at developing an integrated theory of family violence. We wanted a theory that was applicable to child abuse, wife abuse, and the hidden forms of intimate violence. One attempt to develop an integrated theory failed miserably when the resulting model was so complex that we had a hard time following it ourselves when we had to proofread the figure for a book in which it was to be published. While we wanted to borrow the best and most useful elements from the theories we reviewed, this seemed to be impossible.

As a consequence, we turned to trying to develop a more "middle range" (Merton, 1945) theory. Exchange or choice theory seemed to be a framework that best integrated the key elements of the diverse theories. Moreover, exchange theory also had the virtue of providing a suitable perspective to explain and answer a variety of questions and issues in the study of family violence, such as "Why do battered women remain with violent men?"

And so, we responded to the newspaper reporter by stating: "People hit and abuse family members because *they can.*"

The reporter was quite taken aback. He wanted a simple statement, but this seemed too simple. To better understand what it implies, and why it is not simple at all, one has to know and appreciate some of the key assumptions of exchange theory.

Key Assumptions of Exchange Theory

An assumption of exchange theory that is relevant in explaining family violence is that human interaction is guided by the pursuit of rewards and the avoidance of punishment and costs. In addition, an individual who supplies reward services to another obliges him or her to fulfill an obligation, and thus the second individual must furnish benefits to the first (Blau, 1964). If reciprocal exchange of rewards occurs, the interaction will continue. But if reciprocity is not received, the interaction will be broken off.

Intrafamilial relations are more complex than those studied by traditional exchange theorists. In some instances it is not feasible or possible to break off interaction, even if there is not reciprocity. When the "principle of distributive justice" is violated, there can be increased anger, resentment, conflict, and violence.

Many students of family violence tend to view violence as the last resort to solving problems in the family. Nye (1979), however, notes that this need not be the case. Spanking, for instance, is frequently the first choice of action by many parents.

When we say that *people hit family members because they can*, we are applying the basic assumptions of exchange theory to the case of family violence. We expect that people will only use violence toward family members when the costs of being violent do not outweigh the rewards.

There are a variety of costs for being violent. First, there is the potential that the victim will hit back. Second, a violent assault could lead to the arrest and/or imprisonment of the person who has done the hitting. Using violence could also lead to a loss of status. Finally, too much violence might lead to the dissolution of the family. Thus there are potential significant costs involved in being violent.

Social control is a means of raising the costs of violent behavior. Police intervention, criminal charges, imprisonment, loss of status, and loss of income are all forms of social control that could raise the costs and lower the rewards of violent behavior.

From these basic assumptions, we find that there are certain structural properties of families that make them violence prone, and there are specific family and individual traits that make certain families more at risk for violence than other families.

Inequality, Privacy, Social Controls, and Violence

We can expand our first proposition that people hit family members because they can into three propositions:

(1) Family members are more likely to use violence in the home when they expect the costs of being violent to be less than the rewards.

(2) The absence of effective social controls (e.g., police intervention) over family relations decreases the costs of one family member being violent toward another.

(3) Certain social and family structures reduce social control in family relations and, therefore, reduce the costs and increase the rewards of being violent.

Inequality in the home can both reduce the social control and reduce the costs of being violent. The *private nature* of the modern family serves to reduce the degree of social control exercised over family relations (Laslett, 1978, 1973). Finally, the *image of the "real man"* in society also reduces social control in the home and increases the rewards of being violent.

Inequality. The normative power structure in society and the family, and the resulting sexual and generational inequality in the family, serves to reduce the chances that victims of family violence can threaten or inflict harm on offenders. Husbands are typically bigger than wives, have higher-status positions, and earn more money. Because of this, they can use violence without fear of being struck back hard enough to be injured. Moreover, they do not risk having their wives take economic or social sanctions against them. Parents can use violence toward their children without fear that their children can strike back and injure them. The fact that the use of violence toward children by mothers decreases with the child's age (Gelles & Hargreaves, 1981) can be interpreted as a consequence of the greater risk of being hit back as the child grows older and larger. Women and children may be the most frequent victims of family violence because they have no place to run and are not strong enough or do not possess sufficient resources to inflict costs on their attackers.

Privacy. Victims of family violence could turn to outside agencies to redress their grievances, but the private nature of the family reduces the accessibility of outside agencies of social control. Neighbors who report that they overhear incidents of family violence also say that they fear intervening in another person's home. Police, prosecutors, and courts are reluctant to pursue cases involving domestic violence. When these cases are followed up, the courts are faced with the no-win position of either doing nothing or separating the combatants. Thus, to protect a child, judges may view as their only alternative removing the child from the home. To protect the woman, the solution may be a separation or divorce. Either situation puts the legal system in the position of breaking up a family to protect the individual members. Because courts typically view this as a drastic step, such court-ordered separations or removals are comparatively rare, unless there is stark evidence of repeated grievous injury.

Violence and the "real man." One last cost of being violent is the loss of social status that goes along with being labeled a "child beater" or a "wife beater." However, there are subcultures where aggressive sexual and violent behavior is considered proof that someone is a "real man" (Toby, 1966). Thus, rather than risk status loss, violent family members may actually realize a status gain. Moreover, that notion that "a man's home is his castle" reduces external social control over family life.

In situations where status can be lost by being violent, individuals employ accepted vocabularies of motive (Mills, 1940) or "accounts" (Lyman & Scott, 1970) to explain their behavior. Thus violent fathers or mothers might explain their actions by saying they were drunk or lost control. Parents who shared the same desire to batter their children might nod in agreement without realizing that a real loss of control would have produced a much more grievous injury or even death.

Applying Exchange/Social Control Theory

An exchange/social control theory approach to family violence can be extremely helpful in explaining some of the patterns of family violence that have been uncovered in recent empirical investigations.

The child abuse literature notes that certain types of children are at greater risk for abuse. Ill, handicapped, premature, ugly, and demanding children are at greater risk of being abused by their parents. These children either make great demands on their parents (economically, socially, or psychologically) or, as in the case of deformed children or children seen as ugly by their parents, may be perceived as not providing sufficient gratification in return for the parents' investment of time and energy. In any case, when a parent perceives the costs of parenting to outweigh the rewards, the alternatives are limited. The relationship between parent and child is difficult to break—with the exception of giving the child up for adoption or foster care, or the death of a child or parent. Thus, in the case of few alternatives and high dissatisfaction, the parent may resort to violence or abuse.

A similar combination of lack of alternatives and imbalance of effort invested and rewards received may be helpful in understanding other violent family relationships. Also, it is important not to lose sight of the fact that violence itself may be rewarding. Exchange theorists note that to inflict "costs" on someone who has injured you may be rewarding. The idea of "revenge being sweet" can be used to explain why wives resort to severe forms of violence in response to being punched or hit by their husbands. Also, children who assault parents who were violent, and middle-aged women who assault their elderly mothers (who may have been violent when younger), are examples of this principle of exchange theory.

The sociologist F. Ivan Nye (1979) has applied exchange theory to family violence and developed a number of theoretical propositions. First, he stated:

> Violence in the family is more frequent in societies that have no legal or other normative structure prohibiting it. In societies that prohibit violence against some members (wives) but permit it against others (children), violence will be less frequent toward those members against whom it is prohibited than toward those against whom it is allowed.

Nye goes on to propose that wife beating and child beating are less common in families that have relatives and/or friends nearby, while child beating is more common in single-parent than in two-parent families. We would recast his propositions to read:

> Family violence is more common when nonnuclear family members (e.g., friends, relatives, bystanders) are unavailable, unable, or unwilling to be part of the daily system of family interaction, and thus unable to serve as agents of formal and informal social control.

In terms of the general pattern of relationships among family members, the greater the disparity between perceived investment in a family relationship such as parenting, and the perceived returns on the investment, the greater the likelihood that there will be violence. Parents who abuse teenage children (and risk being hit back) may do so because they may believe that their investment in rearing the children has yielded disappointing results.

These propositions again tend to view violence as a last resort or final alternative to an imbalance of investment and rewards in family relations. It is important to note that violence could be the first resort. Spanking children may be common because it is culturally approved and because it is immediately gratifying to the parent. Many parents justify their use of violence as a child-rearing technique because it tends to bring with it immediate emotional reward for the parent and immediate cessation of the child's offending or perceived offending behavior.

Exchange theory is also useful for explaining other findings in the study of family violence. Parents who overestimate their children's ability and capabilities may abuse them because these parents expect more out of the relationship with the children than they receive.

TOWARD PREVENTING AND TREATING FAMILY VIOLENCE

One of the virtues of an exchange/social control theory of family violence is that it has direct applications to the prevention and treatment of intimate violence. Again, to oversimplify, if violence occurs in families because family members *can* be violent, then the goal of prevention and treatment is to make it so they cannot. To do this requires practitioners and social policy planners to consider how they can increase the degree of social control over families, raise the costs of violence, and reduce the rewards. The final chapter of this text considers programs and policies that are designed to treat violent families as well as prevent violence before it can occur.

DISCUSSION QUESTIONS

(1) Why would it be improper and perhaps even harmful to use the profiles of violent families presented in this chapter to predict which families will abuse children or spouses?
(2) How does the private nature of the family contribute to both love and violence within families?
(3) What are some of the "rewards" of being violent in families?

SUGGESTED ASSIGNMENTS

(1) Design model legislation for either child abuse or wife abuse that would raise the costs of violence in families.
(2) Assume that you have been asked to testify before a state legislature or Congress on the topic of preventing family violence. Based on the theories that attempt to explain family violence, what would you recommend? Prepare your testimony.

Prevention and Treatment: Society's Response and Responsibility

IF PEOPLE ARE VIOLENT toward family members because they can be violent, because the advantages of violence outweigh the costs, because the privacy of the family and social attitudes decrease social control, then how do we break the cycle of violence? How do we protect victims of violence? More important, how can we prevent violence from occurring? We concluded the previous chapter by stating that the goal of prevention and treatment is to make it so people can't be violent. But what does this mean? What programs and policies will make it so people can't be violent? What should we do?

Initially, the response to family violence was to assume that abusive family members were mentally ill. But over the past two decades the tendency to diagnose the causes of violence as a psychological abnormality or mental illness has declined. We realize now that individual psychiatric care for violent family members is but one limited treatment for the problem. Because the roots of family violence lie in the structure of the family and society, we know that individual psychiatric treatment can be effective with only a small number of cases of violence and abuse. Individual and family counseling are still important steps in intervening in family violence, but a variety of programs and policies have been developed that deal with other structural sources of violence. We begin this chapter by reviewing the steps that have been taken to aid in discovering private violence. Over the past two decades, laws have been passed and policies have been implemented by the criminal justice system to help recognize and identify various forms of family violence. But recognition and identification of violence and abuse are but the first step in treating and preventing violence in the home. Intervening once an instance of violence is publicly identified poses an important problem. Should we respond with efforts to *control* violence in the home, or should our approach be one of *compassion?* We examine the dilemma of compassion versus control in the next section. The following section reviews the various treatment programs that have been developed to deal with various types of family violence. Finally, the chapter concludes with a discussion of prevention, and we present a number of important steps that should be taken if we want to reduce the tragic toll of family violence in society.

FROM BEHIND CLOSED DOORS: RECOGNIZING FAMILY VIOLENCE

Child Abuse: Reporting Laws

Because violence was hidden behind the closed doors of the American household for so many years, one of the initial policy approaches was to make sure that abuse and violence were recognized publicly so that human service professionals could respond with the proper treatment. In the first decade after child abuse was recognized as a significant health and social problem, a great amount of effort went into assuring that abused children would be identified and responded to with the proper treatment. Between 1962 and 1970, all 50 states enacted mandatory child abuse reporting laws that required designated professionals to report suspected cases of child abuse. Mandatory reporting laws were designed to bring child abuse out from behind closed doors. There are many professionals who see children daily and who see the visible and emotional signs of abuse and neglect. However, prior to the enactment of reporting laws, many professionals, including physicians and teachers, were extremely reluctant to report cases of child abuse. The reasons for failing to report were many and varied. Some professionals were unaware of the signs of abuse and often accepted the explanation that the bruises and scars were the results of accidents. Even if the signs of abuse were clearly identifiable (for instance, a hand mark on the side of the face), professionals were still reluctant to become involved in what most people considered to be a "family matter." Fear of being sued for false accusation also played a part in failure to report. Finally, professionals and the public alike frequently did not know to whom to report cases of abuse.

Gradually, state laws were drafted that mandated specific professionals (or, in some states, all adults) to report suspected abuse. In order to protect people who made reports in good faith, state statutes provided that people making reports in good faith could not be sued for false accusation. When it appeared that the early versions of the law still were not generating adequate numbers of reports, some states added criminal penalties for failing to report cases of suspected abuse. In addition to passing laws, states also engaged in public awareness campaigns and public education programs. The initial impact of such campaigns was startling. Florida began one of the first public awareness programs in the early 1970s. Along with the program, Florida provided a toll-free number for people to call and report suspected cases of abuse. Reports of child abuse in Florida before the public awareness campaign were fewer than 20 per year. In the first year after the campaign, there were 25,000 reports of suspected abuse!

Wife Abuse: Criminalization

Wives were treated differently than children. Because most people assume that adult women are capable of reporting their own victimization, there were no calls for implementing reporting laws for battered women. Yet women still had the problem of being victimized behind closed doors. If the shame and stigma of being a battered wife were not bad enough, many state laws actually stipulated that, for a wife to charge her husband with assault and battery, she had to be more severely injured than someone who was assaulted by a stranger. The criminal justice system, beginning with the role and actions of the police, traditionally approached wife abuse from various perspectives—denial, acceptance, lack of awareness, and helplessness. Some police departments used "stitch rules" to respond to cases of domestic assault—a wife who was abused had to require a certain number of surgical sutures before a husband could be arrested for assault and battery (Field & Field, 1973). Prosecutors frequently failed to take the complaints of battered women seriously and sent women home with the advice that they should "kiss and make up."

Many law enforcement officials who tried to assist battered wives complained that the wives themselves handcuffed the criminal justice system. Police frequently point out that women attack and even kill police officers who are called on to intervene in domestic violence. Other police officers point to the numerous instances where women who have been beaten fail to file charges against their husbands or withdraw the charges within a few days of the violent episode. Some prosecutors also point out that women frequently fail to follow through in pressing charges. Some women have actually dropped charges at the trial, and one announced that "husbands are supposed to hit their wives, aren't they?" (Parnas, 1967).

Statements such as the one that claims that husbands are supposed to hit their wives create a kind of self-fulfilling prophecy where people and prosecutors expect that all battered women will fail to follow through with legal actions. Consequently, police and prosecutors often advise victims against taking legal action. As a result, police and district attorneys are seen as less than sympathetic to the problem of battered women. Organized women's groups spent much of the 1970s seeking equal protection for battered women. Class action suits were filed to assure that police and prosecutors paid attention to the problem of battered women. In December 1976, women in New York City filed a class action suit against the New York Police Department, probation officers, and family court employees for failing to prosecute abusive husbands. The police settled out of court in 1977. In 1974, a class action suit was filed against Cleveland district attorneys for denying battered women equal protection under the law by not following through in prosecution of abusive husbands. That suit was settled by a consent decree ordering prosecutors to change their practices. In Oakland, the police were accused of illegal conduct because of their pattern and practice of discouraging arrests in cases of domestic violence. (See "Battered Women Press Police," 1979, for complete details on the above legal procedures.) In all these class action suits, the central goal was to eliminate selective inattention to the problem of battered women and to "criminalize" violence against women.

At the beginning of the 1970s few states had laws aimed at reducing spousal violence. Today, most states have enacted legislation on domestic violence. Most of the state laws created new civil and criminal legal remedies for persons abused by family or household members.

Some state laws specify the powers and duties of the police and courts in handling domestic violence. Some laws mandate social agencies to provide services to violent families. Finally, a number of states have enacted laws that provide funding for battered wife shelters.

Hidden Violence: Few Legal Remedies

The legal remedies that were applied to child abuse and spousal violence have, in general, not been specifically aimed at the hidden forms of family violence. Adolescent victims of violence are technically covered by child abuse statutes, but, as we saw in Chapter 5, adolescents are rarely reported as victims of physical child abuse. Sibling violence is covered only by normal laws pertaining to criminal assault. This, too, is the case for violence toward parents. The only exception to this pattern is that 42 states have enacted reporting laws aimed at victims of elderly abuse.

INTERVENTION IN FAMILY VIOLENCE: COMPASSION OR CONTROL

Once a case of child or wife abuse has been reported and recognized, the next important step is to intervene. What should be done? As we have noted numerous times in this book, the first emotional reaction to child abuse is to call for stiff and harsh penalties to be meted out against abusive parents. In addition to punishing parents, people frequently advise that the children should be taken away from abusive parents. Similarly, removal of elderly victims of abuse from the homes of their abusers is considered an important first step in treating elder abuse.

The physicians Alvin Rosenfeld and Eli Newberger (1977) have noted two competing philosophies that have been applied to treating child abuse. These philosophies are equally applicable to other forms of family violence treatment.

On one hand is the compassionate approach to abuse. Human service professionals who treat violence and abuse from this perspective approach it with an abundance of human kindness and a nonpunitive outlook on intervention. The compassionate philosophy views the abusive parents as victims themselves. The cause of the abuse may be seen in social and developmental origins, and not in the abuser. Abusive parents, rather than being seen as cold, cruel monsters, are seen as sad, deprived, and needy human beings. Compassionate intervention involves supporting the abuser and his or her family. Homemaker services, health and child care, and other supports are made available to the family.

On the other hand is the control model. The control model involves aggressive use of intervention to limit, and, if necessary, punish, the deviant violent behavior. The control approach places full responsibility for actions with the abuser. Control involves removal of the child from the home, arrest of an abusive husband (or wife), and full criminal prosecution of the offender.

The compassion model has dangers for the clinician and the family. The compassionate clinician may strive to support a family and may actually raise the risk of further violence by relieving the offender of responsibility. A clinician's concern for alienating abusive parents or abusive partners may compromise the clinician's judgment and result in a victim being left at risk. In addition, should the compassionate approach fail to result in positive change, the human service professional may be left feeling demoralized and burned out.

Human service professionals are reluctant to use the control approach, even when the situation literally screams out for action. Clinicians have been heard to say that they were reluctant to use stern measures because "the family has already suffered enough." Sadly, on some occasions, a control approach may actually raise the risks for abused children and women. On one occasion in the state of Rhode Island, a child was removed from a mother who was neglecting the child. The child was placed in a foster home, only to be beaten to death six months later by the foster father. When women flee battering relationships for shelter, this sometimes enrages the husband to the point of homicide, as happened once to a woman in Boston who was attacked and killed by her husband a few blocks from the shelter.

There is no easy solution to the control/compassion dilemma. Rosenfeld and Newberger (1977) call for giving compassion *and* control. Assessment and intervention functions should probably be performed by separate individuals. A control approach might be used in assessment, while compassion is reserved for use once the proper course of treatment is prescribed for the family. In the best of all possible worlds, the choice of intervention would not boil down to a choice between protecting the child or woman by removal versus keeping the family together. The best of all possible worlds would involve appropriate measures of legal control and humane support. The following section reviews the standard and useful forms of treatment that have been developed for dealing with domestic violence.

TREATMENT

As we saw in the previous section, any program or policy designed to treat the problem of violence between family members must be capable of *protecting* the victim(s) while preventing further violence—if possible by strengthening the family. Without both of these components, there is no long-term solution to violence in the home.

Treating Child Abuse

Identification and reporting. The first step in treating child abuse is to identify children in need of services. Consequently, considerable effort has been devoted to improving techniques of identifying and reporting cases of child abuse to the proper human service agencies. Such steps involve a variety of efforts, which are coordinated among numerous public and private agencies. First, as we already mentioned, all 50 states enacted legislation that required reporting suspected cases of child abuse. In order to assure that cases would and could be properly identified, public and private agencies engaged in training programs to educate potential reporters about the signs of abuse. These public education and awareness programs greatly increased the number of child abuse reports that were generated. Because of this, states and localities established child abuse hot lines that were staffed 24 hours per day. These hot lines were designed to receive reports. Soon states found that they also required 24-hour-a-day response capabilities.

Child welfare services. It should be obvious from the discussion of the incidence of child abuse in Chapter 3 that if all cases of child abuse and violence toward children were reported to public and private social welfare agencies, and if each reported case was fully investigated and provided services, it would tax the existing social welfare system beyond its present means. In many, if not most, states, child welfare or protective service workers are already burdened with caseloads that are far too large to allow the workers to service the child and family adequately—and this is when people estimate that only one of three child abuse cases is being reported! Some caseworkers have caseloads of 30 to even 50 families, whereas most professionals in the field of social and human services believe that protective workers should serve no more than 20 families at a time.

The optimal situation for child welfare agencies is to be able to respond to problems of child abuse quickly, effectively, and in a manner that treats the causes of abuse, not just the symptoms. Child welfare systems need to be able to provide immediate crisis intervention when children are at risk. In Florida, only 25% of reported cases of child abuse are responded to within the first 24 hours (Straus, Gelles, & Steinmetz, 1980). This is too slow to protect many of the victims of child abuse. Ideally, a protective service system ought to be able to respond to all reports of child abuse and neglect and be able to supply emergency resources for the child and family immediately, or at least within 24 hours of the report.

The nature of the child welfare response is even more important than how fast the response can be made. Professionals in the field of child protection recommend that child welfare agencies are able to provide emergency homemaker services, a hot line to help parents deal with day-to-day crises, transportation, child care services, counseling or referrals for professional counseling, health care, clothing and shelter, access to self-help groups such as Parents Anonymous, and other resources that ease the burden of child care for parents.

Education for parenting. Studies of child abuse often show that violent and abusive parents do not know how to manage or cope with child rearing. Frequently, abusive parents do not understand the basic stages of child development and have unrealistic expectations of their children's abilities. Experience shows that an important treatment and prevention technique is to provide educational services so that parents can learn about child development and appropriate discipline techniques (Jeffrey, 1976; Kempe & Helfer, 1974).

Summary. A complete discussion of treating child abuse would require an entire book. We have only provided an overview of the various problems and options available for treatment. One obvious facet of treating child abuse is that, because there are multiple causes of abuse, we require multiple services and interventions. Multiservice and multidiscipline teams have been helpful in treating child abuse. It is important to remember that some treatments will be effective for certain families and fail miserably with other families. Parents Anonymous chapters have an outstanding success rate, but only for those parents who choose to participate. Providing dental or health care services might be sufficient to relieve stress on one household but might not be adequate for another family.

Currently, one major problem in providing adequate treatment is dollars and cents. Most state protective service agencies simply do not have the resources to deal with the number of cases of child abuse and neglect that are being reported. Agencies are trying to add professional staff, but, frequently, these staff are inadequately trained to deal with the complex and emotional problems they confront once on the job. In some states, protective service workers have fewer than 40 hours of training! A number of states do not even require that protective service workers hold a professional degree.

The goal of protective service is to best serve the child and family. Optimally, this would involve providing the proper mixture of support services and professional counseling to help the family provide adequate care for its children. When such services are rejected by the family or are ineffective, child welfare professionals face the problem of removing the child from the home and finding a suitable placement for the child. Here we come to another can of worms. Locating an adequate placement is a tremendously difficult and complex task. Abused children frequently require more care and attention than the average child. They may have special physical or emotional needs. This can be extremely taxing on a foster family. Because foster families are frequently at a premium, protective workers sometimes find that they are placing a child in a home that has not been adequately screened or assessed. Sometimes, sadly, this places the child at increased risk.

Ultimately, even the best protective service system is one that can only react to cases of child abuse. Adequately treating child abuse may prevent further abuse in that home, but it can never prevent abuse that has already taken place. We will turn to prevention in the final section of the chapter.

Treating Wife Abuse

Treating wife abuse involves different services and different institutions than those brought to bear to ameliorate the problem of child abuse. Because the victims of wife abuse are adults, conventional wisdom leads one to assume that they are able to take care of themselves and are not helpless victims of violence. There are only a few mandatory reporting laws for wife abuse. Few agencies even bother to keep records of cases of wife abuse. Police records note wife abuse either as "domestic disturbances" or, rarely, as "assault." Hospitals rarely separate cases of wife assault from other emergency cases. There are some adult protective units in social service agencies, but they typically focus their attention on dependent or vulnerable adults—for instance, the elderly.

The main crisis intervention services that victims of wife abuse can turn to are the police, courts, and battered wife shelters.

The police. Family disturbance calls have been labeled the "common cold" of police work (Elliot, 1989). These calls, many of which involve violence between spouses, constitute the largest single category of calls received by police departments each year (Police Foundation, 1977). The American police officer frequently functions as the neighborhood social worker. In cases of child abuse, police are often called upon to intervene in ongoing instances of violence or neglect of children, and their primary function in these instances is to report the abuse or neglect to the proper child welfare authorities. But, in cases of wife abuse, the police not only are the first on the scene of ongoing violence, they are also the agents of social control who command the primary power to protect the victims of wife abuse.

The sociologists Sarah Berk and Donileen Loseke (1980) note that "as front-line agents of social control in domestic disturbances, police are the proximate representative of state policy." The alternative social services that are available to women (such as shelters) most often depend on the police for cooperation—police must inform family violence victims of the availability of these services. The police are a crucial link between the victim of wife abuse and treatment programs available in her community.

Police intervention in cases of domestic violence is dangerous work. As we noted earlier, as many police officers are killed answering domestic disturbance calls as are killed pursuing armed robbers. Domestic disturbance calls are among the least glamorous and least prestigious types of work officers do. Few officers receive medals or promotions because they are effective in handling domestic violence calls.

Because family violence calls are extremely dangerous *and* the rewards are few, police are rarely motivated to get involved in treatment or prevention. Students of family violence have been quite critical of the traditional police reluctance to intervene and ameliorate family violence (Dobash & Dobash, 1979; Field & Field, 1973).

Berk and Loseke (1980) studied the factors that influenced police officers' decisions on how to intervene in wife assault. Examining data from 262 official police reports concerning domestic disturbances in Santa Barbara, California, Berk and Loseke found four factors that were related to whether or not police decided to arrest a violent husband. If the wife-victim signed an arrest warrant, if both husband and wife were present when the police arrived, if the wife alleged that violence had occurred, and if the husband was drunk when the police arrived—all raised the likelihood that an arrest would be made. However, if the wife made the original call to the police, this actually reduced the chances that the husband would be arrested. Thus the traditional complaint that police do not effectively intervene because they, as an occupational group, support the right of husbands to hit their wives and the complaint that the police are reluctant to get involved in "family matters" do not seem to hold under analysis. The data suggest that situational factors, not occupational attitudes, affect police decision making.

In the last few years, the treatment of choice for the criminal justice "common cold" has changed from apparent indifference or compassionate mediation to firmer control and mandatory or "presumptive" arrest. A number of factors have led to a wide-scale adoption of control strategies for dealing with family violence and, more specifically, violence toward wives. One important factor was the feminist and women's movement argument that the criminal justice system was indifferent to wife abuse. Those advancing this argument claimed that the criminal justice system, especially the police, treated intimate violence differently than instances of stranger assault. Critics claimed that the police assign domestic disturbance calls a low priority, do not respond or delay response to these categories of calls, and avoid arrest or use of other control strategies in favor of simply restoring order or calming the violent parties down.

A second major factor that moved police departments toward a control approach and adopting mandatory or presumptive arrest strategies was the publication of the results of the Minneapolis Police Experiment (Sherman & Berk, 1984). This study, funded by the

National Institute of Justice and conducted by the Police Foundation, called for the police in two precincts in Minneapolis to randomly assign violent family offenders to one of three experimental conditions: arrest, separation, or advice/mediation. Eligible households were those where both offender and victim were present when the police arrived and where the nature of the incident was classified as "misdemeanor assault." A six-month period followed the experimental condition during which interviews were conducted with victims and offenders. Official records of subsequent incidents of family violence were also collected. An analysis of the follow-up data indicated that those receiving the arrest intervention had the lowest rate of recidivism (10%) and those who were separated had the highest (24%). Advice and mediation cases had a 19% recidivism rate. The public announcement and subsequent publication of the results of the Minneapolis Police Experiment led a number of large urban police departments to adopt mandatory or presumptive arrest interventions in cases of domestic assault.

A third factor that led to the adoption of arrest strategies was the publication of the U.S. Attorney General's Task Force on Family Violence report (Department of Justice, 1984a). Drawing heavily from the results of the Minneapolis Police Experiment, this report called for police departments and criminal justice agencies to recognize family violence as criminal activity and respond accordingly. The report recommended arrest as the preferred strategy for responding to cases of family violence.

A fourth factor may have been the case of *Tracy Thurman v. the City of Torrington, Connecticut.* Thurman was a battered wife who had frequently sought help from the Torrington police to protect her from the violent attacks of her estranged husband. Thurman was badly battered and left permanently injured in June 1983 and subsequently filed a civil suit against the City of Torrington and 29 police officers (*Thurman v. City of Torrington,* 595 F. Supp. 1521; *Thurman v. City of Torrington,* USDC. No. H-84120, June 25, 1985). Thurman was awarded 2.3 million dollars and later settled out of court for 1.9 million dollars. The threat of similar suits motivated a number of eastern municipalities to adopt the policy of mandatory arrest for cases of family violence.

There are a number of important problems with both the assumptions and the evidence that appear to support the adoption of arrest as the strategy of choice in dealing with violent couples. The first problem is the assumption that police are reluctant to arrest husbands who assault their wives. Students of wife assault and feminists have argued that rates of arrest in cases of intimate violence are lower than the rates of arrest for stranger assault and that this reveals a bias in the criminal justice system. The criminologist Delbert Elliot (1989) has reviewed the data that compare the rates of arrest for family and nonfamily assaults and found that the arrest rate for stranger violence is not significantly higher than the arrest rate for family violence. This finding may undermine the claim that there is bias in police practice. On the other hand, assuming that it is more difficult to arrest strangers involved in assaults, one might have expected the rate of arrest for family assaults to be much higher than for stranger assaults. Thus Elliot's data could be used to support the claim that a bias against arrest exists for cases of family violence. A third possible interpretation is that police generally avoid arrest in all cases of violence.

A second significant problem concerns the internal and external validity of the Minneapolis Police Experiment, which has been cited as supporting presumptive arrest. The internal validity problems include questions about the degree to which the treatment was truly based on random assignment. Officers could have violated the assumptions of random assignment by either avoiding a domestic disturbance call or classifying a call "felony assault" or "non-misdemeanor" violence. Another problem of internal validity arises because the vast majority of the cases in the study were the results of the work of only a few police officers in two precincts. In addition, the authors had significant problems with missing data. Without sophisticated statistical procedures to deal with the problems of missing data, the investigators would have had too few cases for valid analysis.

Finally, a replication of the Minneapolis Police Experiment conducted in Omaha, Nebraska, failed to find that arrest reduced the rate of repeated violence in cases of wife abuse (Dunford, Huizinga, & Elliot, 1989). The Omaha study did find that arrest did not raise the risk for battered women—in other words, arrested husbands did not increase their level of violence. One unexpected outcome of the Omaha experiment was that, in cases when the violent husbands or cohabitants were not present when the police arrived and police issued arrest warrants, these men did reduce their use of violence toward their partners. Thus, while arrest itself did not deter violent men, the *threat* of arrest was a deterrent.

Additional replications of the Minneapolis experiment are now under way and results will be published shortly. At the moment, scientific evidence is split over the actual effectiveness of arrest as a deterrent to wife abuse.

The courts. The second line of defense for an adult victim of domestic violence is the court system. Court-imposed intervention includes the issuance of protective orders or restraining orders to keep violent husbands out of the home and away from their wives and children. Peace bonds are frequently imposed along with these orders to add the deterrent effect of money lost should the order be violated. Prosecution for less than lethal family violence is still problematic, and the courts still retain vestiges of viewing domestic violence as "family matters."

Only a tiny fraction of incidents of marital violence reach a courtroom. Of the more than 800 homes that reported some form of marital violence in the last year surveyed by Gelles and Straus for the Second National Family Violence Survey (1988), 5 (about .5 of 1%) went to court. This number constitutes a mere 13% of those cases of violence in which the police were called. The few cases of spouse assault that ended up in court resulted in a variety of actions. These actions included dismissing the charges, warning the abuser, requiring the abuser to enter counseling, fining the abuser, jail, or a suspended sentence. Respondents indicated a wide range of satisfaction with the results of their appearances in court: 3 in 10 were very satisfied; 7% were somewhat satisfied; nearly 20% were somewhat dissatisfied; nearly 8 in 100 were very dissatisfied—however, the largest percentage, more than one-third (36.1), said they were not sure.

Shelters. Perhaps the most important development in the last 20 years in treating wife abuse has been the grass-roots development of battered wife shelters or safe houses. One of the first shelters designed to protect victims of family violence was created almost by accident. As we mentioned in Chapter 2, in 1971, a group of women in Chiswick, England, met to discuss rising food prices. But prices were not their biggest complaint--loneliness was. Out of these first meetings a Women's Aid project was established by Erin Pizzey. Soon a house was set up as Chiswick Women's Aid. The house became a center for women with personal problems. Before long, the house filled up with women with a common problem—wife abuse. Within three years, Women's Aid of Chiswick became the model for women's shelters around the world.

In 1976, there were probably no more than five or six shelters in the United States. By 1990, there may well be over 1,000, and the list grows every day. Some shelters are actually the result of class projects organized by students enrolled in family violence courses at colleges and universities. Nearly every shelter was established through volunteer effort and donations. Few, if any, shelters were blessed with government or foundation funding. Budgets are typically small, furniture donated, and staff time volunteered.

The concept of a shelter, safe house, or refuge is quite simple and solves a basic problem for the battered wife—it provides her and her children a place to go. Because wife abuse and family violence often happen on weekends, at nights, or in the dead of winter, there is frequently no place a victim can turn for help (except the police). Battered wives in bathrobes have spent hours walking the freezing streets. Shelters provide protection for the victim or potential victim of a violent assault. In addition, shelters often make referrals for legal and marriage counseling, help women find jobs, and, above all, help restore the sense of self-esteem that women have typically lost after years of psychological and physical battering.

Shelters have various capabilities, abilities, and rules. Some can hold 30 women; some can hold but a few. Most women seem to stay for a week or two before they leave. Researchers report that anywhere from one-third to two-thirds of the women who come to shelters do not return to their violent mate (Giles-Sims, 1983; Sedlak, 1988).

There have been a handful of systematic studies of the impact and effect of shelters. Andrea Sedlak (1988) reports that women who stayed in shelters for nontrivial periods of time (three weeks) evidenced decreases in depression and increased independence from their abusers. The sociologist Jean Giles-Sims (1983) studied 31 women who sought help from a shelter. She interviewed 24 of these women six months after they left the shelter and found that the shelter had beneficial effects by helping to empower the victims. Of course, this is a small sample with no comparison group, so one can neither generalize from this research nor attribute the changes to the shelter. Other studies that examined the impact of shelters suffer from the same methodological problems and cannot be used to determine whether women who return to their husbands after a shelter stay are at greater or lesser risk for abuse.

A recent study by the sociologists Richard Berk, Phyllis Newton, and Sarah Fenstermaker Berk (1986) followed 243 wife battery victims in Santa Barbara, California. At the end of 18 months they were still in contact with 155 of the victims. Using the records from a shelter, the researchers were able to determine which of the 243 victims had stayed in a shelter between the time of the first and second interviews. A total of 57 women had used a shelter, staying between 1 and 30 days. Based on their interviews, the investigators concluded that shelters appear to have a beneficial effect. However, the benefits depend on the attitudes of the women. When a victim can actually take control of her life, a shelter stay can dramatically reduce the likelihood of new violence. More than 8 of the 10 women who stayed at a shelter experienced no new violence between leaving the shelter and being interviewed (an average of 54 days). For women who cannot take control of their lives, shelters either have no impact or, worse, may actually trigger retaliation from an angry partner or husband: 5% of the women who left the shelter were beaten more than once after returning home.

Berk and his associates caution that theirs is but a single study with some important methodological limitations. It would be premature, the researchers argue, to base major policy changes on this single study. The study does, however, illuminate the fact that the impact of shelters is not uniform for all victims of wife battery.

Men's groups. Since 1980, there have been a number of men's counseling groups established with the purpose of counseling violent men. Emerge in Boston, Brother to Brother in Providence, Rhode Island, and a number of other organizations around the country have been organized by men with the goal of counseling violent men.

Voluntary group counseling programs tend to have few men enrolled and dropout rates that range from one-third to two-thirds (Saunders & Hanusa, 1986). Follow-up studies of volunteer programs tend to find nonviolence rates of between two-thirds and three-quarters (Gondolf, 1987). A court-mandated program studied by Donald Dutton (1986) followed 50 male participants in a group program for male batterers and found recidivism rates as low as 4%. There are many significant methodological problems with many of these evaluation studies, so the positive results that are reported should be viewed as suggestive and not definitive proof that these programs are effective in treating violent men.

Other Forms of Family Violence

As we noted in Chapter 5, violent relations other than parent to child and husband to wife have long been hidden from public attention. Thus, with only rare exceptions, there are few treatment programs for sibling violence and violence toward parents (with the exception of violence toward the elderly). If these forms of violence are recognized and treated at all, they typically are dealt with through traditional individual and family counseling.

Mandatory elder abuse reporting laws exist in 42 states. The laws vary from state to state and the results have been mixed. Funding and staffing for mandatory adult protective service laws are often quite limited. Adult protective service workers have found that elderly victims of violence have been extremely reluctant to leave violent and abusive homes. The fear of being institutionalized seems to outweigh the pain and suffering some elderly people experience. Thus adult protective service workers often invest countless hours investigating reports of elder abuse only to find the victim reluctant to accept any form of treatment.

To our knowledge, there are only a limited number of self-help groups for victims of elder abuse. Most parents still seem to be suffering in silence and shame. Violent siblings, unless they maim or kill a brother or sister, are not even recognized as violent, let alone attended to with treatment or intervention.

One of the roadblocks to effective treatment for the hidden forms of family violence is the fact that child abuse and wife abuse were recognized and treated by completely separate institutions and systems. There is little, if any, overlap in the treatment programs aimed at either child or wife abuse. There is little recognition of the problem of *family violence*. Each group identifies their own problems, develops their own treatment, secures their own funds, and, in an era of scarce money for social services, jealously guards their own turf. One of the notable gaps in the entire treatment program is a recognition of the problem of family violence and the development of treatment modalities for the whole family and the entire range of the problem.

PREVENTION

Treatment is necessary to protect the lives and welfare of the victims or potential victims of family violence. But even the implementation of effective and efficient treatment programs will not break the cycle of cultural norms and values that contributes to the violent nature of the family. Nor do treatment programs alone alter the characteristics of society and the family that increase the risk that certain families will be violent and abusive.

The central goal of programs and policies aimed at family violence is to prevent violence. The findings presented in this book clearly point to the fact that some fundamental changes in values and beliefs will have to occur before we see a real decrease in the level of violence in the family. Looking toward the future, there are a number of policy steps that could help prevent intimate violence.

(1) *Eliminate the norms that legitimize and glorify violence in the society and the family.* The elimination of spanking as a child-rearing technique, the promotion of gun control to get deadly weapons out of the home, the elimination of corporal punishment in school and the death penalty, and an elimination of media violence that glorifies and legitimizes violence are all necessary steps. In short, we need to cancel the hitting license in society.

(2) *Reduce violence-provoking stress created by society.* Reducing poverty, inequality, and unemployment and providing for adequate housing, feeding, medical and dental care, and educational opportunities are steps that could reduce stress in families.

(3) *Integrate families into a network of kin and community.* Reducing social isolation would be a significant step to help reduce stress and increase the abilities of families to manage stress.

(4) *Change the sexist character of society.* Sexual inequality, perhaps more than economic inequality, makes violence possible in homes. The elimination of men's work and women's work would be a major step toward equality in and out of the home.

(5) *Break the cycle of violence in the family.* This step repeats the message of step 1—violence cannot be prevented as long as we are taught that it is appropriate to hit the people we love. Physical punishment of children is perhaps the most effective means of teaching violence, and eliminating it would be an important step in violence prevention.

Such steps require long-term changes in the fabric of society. These proposals call for such fundamental change in families and family life that many people resist them and argue that they could not work or would ruin the family. The alternative, of course, is that not making such changes continues the harmful and deadly tradition of family violence.

DISCUSSION QUESTIONS

(1) How do police expectations about battered women being prone to drop charges against their abusive husbands create a self-fulfilling prophecy and deny women their proper legal rights of protection?

(2) What legal remedies could be enacted to deal with the problems of hidden family violence—elder abuse, sibling violence, parent abuse, abuse of adolescents?

(3) Give an example of how compassion and control could be used to intervene in cases of child abuse, wife abuse, abuse of the elderly.

SUGGESTED ASSIGNMENT

(1) Create a resource guide that lists the community services (names, addresses, and telephone numbers) of agencies and organizations that deal with various aspects of family violence.

References

Adelson, L. (1972). The battering child. *Journal of the American Medical Association, 222,* 159-161.

Agnew, R., & Huguley, S. (1989). Adolescent violence towards parents. *Journal of Marriage and the Family, 51*(3), 699-711.

Alfaro, J. (1977, July 21-22). *Report on the relationship between child abuse and neglect and later socially deviant behavior.* Paper presented at a symposium, "Exploring the Relationship Between Child Abuse and Delinquency," University of Washington, Seattle.

American Association for Protecting Children. (1989). *Highlights of official child neglect and abuse reporting, 1987.* Denver: American Humane Association.

American Humane Association. (1976). *National analysis of official child neglect and abuse reporting, 1974.* Denver: Author.

American Humane Association. (1980). *National analysis of official child neglect and abuse reporting.* Denver: Author.

American Humane Association. (1984). *Trends in child abuse and neglect: A national perspective.* Denver: Author.

Arias, I., Samios, M., & O'Leary, K. D. (1987). Prevalence and correlates of physical aggression during courtship. *Journal of Interpersonal Violence, 2*(1), 82-90.

Aries, P. (1962). *Centuries of childhood.* New York: Knopf.

Ball, M. (1977). Issues of violence in family casework. *Social Casework, 58,* 3-12.

Bard, M. (1969). Family intervention police teams as a community mental health resource. *Journal of Criminal Law, Criminology, and Police Science, 60*(2), 247-250.

Bard, M. (1971). The study and modification of intra-family violence. In J. L. Singer (Ed.), *The control of aggression and violence* (pp. 149-164). New York: Academic Press.

Bard, M., & Zacker, J. (1971). The prevention of family violence: Dilemmas of community intervention. *Journal of Marriage and the Family, 33*(4), 677-682.

Battered women press police for equal protection. (1979). *Response, 2*(6), 3.

Bender, L. (1959). Children and adolescents who have killed. *American Journal of Psychiatry, 116,* 510-513.

Berk, R., Berk, S. F., Loseke, D. R., & Rauma, D. (1983). Mutual combat and other family violence myths. In D. Finkelhor, R. Gelles, G. Hotaling, & M. Straus (Eds.), *The dark side of families: Current family violence research* (pp. 197-212). Beverly Hills, CA: Sage.

Berk, S., & Loseke, D. (1980). "Handling" family violence: The situated determinants of police arrest in domestic disturbances. *Law and Society Review, 15*(2), 317-346.

Berk, R., Newton, P., & Berk, S. F. (1986). What a difference a day makes: An empirical study of the impact of shelters for battered women. *Journal of Marriage and the Family, 48,* 481-490.

Blau, P. M. (1964). *Exchange and power in social life.* New York: John Wiley.

Block, M., & Sinnott, J. (1979). *Battered elder syndrome: An exploratory study.* Unpublished manuscript, University of Maryland.

Blumberg, M. (1964). When parents hit out. *Twentieth Century, 173,* 39-44.

Boudouris, J. (1971). Homicide and the family. *Journal of Marriage and the Family, 33,* 667-682.

Bowker, L. H. (1983). *Beating wife-beating.* Lexington, MA: Lexington.

Brekke, J., & Saunders, D. (1982). *Research on woman abuse: A review of findings, needs, and issues.* Unpublished manuscript.

Briley, M. (1979). Battered parents. *Dynamic Years, 14,* 24-27.

Bronfenbrenner, U. (1958). Socialization and social class throughout time and space. In E. Maccoby et al. (Eds.), *Readings in social psychology* (pp. 400-425). New York: Holt.

Burgdorf, K. (1980). *Recognition and reporting of child maltreatment.* Rockville, MD: Westat.

Button, A. (1973). Some antecedents of felonious and delinquent behavior. *Journal of Clinical Child Psychology, 2,* 35-38.

Byrd, D. E. (1979). *Intersexual assault: A review of empirical findings.* Paper presented at the annual meetings of the Eastern Sociological Society, New York.

Caffey, J. (1946). Multiple fractures in the long bones of infants suffering from chronic subdural hematoma. *American Journal of Roentgenology, Radium Therapy, and Nuclear Medicine, 58,* 163-173.

Caffey, J. (1957). Some traumatic lesions in growing bones other than fractures and dislocations. *British Journal of Radiology, 23,* 225-238.

Calvert, R. (1974). Criminal and civil liability in husband-wife assaults. In S. Steinmetz & M. Straus (Eds.), *Violence in the family* (pp. 88-90). New York: Harper & Row.

Carr, A. (1977, October 20). *Some preliminary findings on the association between child maltreatment and juvenile misconduct in eight New York counties.* Report to the Administration for Children, Youth and Families, National Center on Child Abuse and Neglect.

Cate, R. M., Henton, J. M., Christopher, F. S., & Lloyd, S. (1982). Premarital abuse: A social psychological perspective. *Journal of Family Issues, 3,* 79-90.

Coleman, D., & Straus, M. (1983). Alcohol abuse and family violence. In E. Gottheil, K. Druley, T. Skoloda, & H. Waxman (Eds.), *Alcohol, drug abuse and aggression* (pp. 104-124). Springfield, IL: Charles C Thomas.

Cornell, C. P., & Gelles, R. J. (1982). Adolescent to parent violence. *Urban Social Change Review, 15,* 8-14.

Curtis, L. (1974). *Criminal violence: National patterns and behavior.* Lexington, MA: Lexington.

D'Agostino, S. (1983, August 17). Finally, judgement. *Worcester Magazine,* pp. 11-13.

Daly, M., & Wilson, M. (1980). Discriminative parental solicitude: A biosocial perspective. *Journal of Marriage and the Family, 42,* 277-288.

Daly, M., & Wilson, M. (1981). Child maltreatment from a sociobiological perspective. *New Directions for Child Development, 11,* 93-112.

Daly, M., & Wilson, M. (1985). Child abuse and other risks of nonliving with both parents. *Ethology and Sociobiology, 6,* 197-210.

Daly, M., & Wilson, M. (1987). Children as homicide victims. In R. J. Gelles & J. B. Lancaster (Eds.), *Child abuse and neglect: Biosocial dimensions* (pp. 201-214). Hawthorne, NY: Aldine de Gruyter.

Daly, M., & Wilson, M. (1988). Evolutionary social psychology and family homicide. *Science, 242,* 524.

Davidson, T. (1978). *Conjugal crime: Understanding and changing the wifebeating pattern.* New York: Hawthorn.

DeMause, L. (Ed.). (1974). *The history of childhood.* New York: Psychohistory Press.

Dietrich, J. N., Starr, R., Jr., & Weisfield, G. E. (1983). Infant maltreatment: Caretaker-infant interaction and developmental consequences at different levels of parenting failure. *Pediatrics, 72*, 532-540.

Dobash, R. E., & Dobash, R. (1979). *Violence against wives.* New York: Free Press.

Dunford, F. W., Huizinga, D., & Elliot, D. S. (1989). *The Omaha Domestic Violence Police Experiment.* Final report to the National Institute of Justice and the City of Omaha, Boulder, CO. (mimeo)

Dutton, D. (1986). The outcome of court-mandated treatment for wife assault: A quasi-experimental evaluation. *Violence and Victims, 1*, 163-176.

Edgerton, R. B. (1981). Foreword. In J. Korbin (Ed.), *Child abuse and neglect: Cross-cultural perspectives* (pp. vii-viii). Berkeley: University of California Press.

Egeland, B., Jacobvitz, D., & Papatola, K. (1987). Intergenerational continuity of abuse. In R. J. Gelles & J. B. Lancaster (Eds.), *Child abuse and neglect: Biosocial dimensions* (pp. 255-276). Hawthorne, NY: Aldine de Gruyter.

Egeland, B., Jacobvitz, D., & Sroufe, A. (1988). Breaking the cycle of abuse. *Child Development, 59*, 1080-1088.

Egeland, B., & Vaughan, B. (1981). Failure of "bond formation" as a cause of abuse, neglect, and maltreatment. *American Journal of Orthopsychiatry, 51*, 78-84.

Elliot, D. S. (1989). Criminal justice procedures in family violence crimes. In L. Ohlin & M. Tonry (Eds.), *Family violence* (pp. 427-480). Chicago: University of Chicago Press.

Elmer, E. (1967). *Children in jeopardy: A study of abused minors and their families.* Pittsburgh: University of Pittsburgh Press.

Erlanger, H. (1974). Social class and corporal punishment in childrearing: A reassessment. *American Sociological Review, 39*, 68-85.

Etzioni, A. (1971). Violence. In R. K. Merton & R. Nisbet (Eds.), *Contemporary social problems* (pp. 709-741). New York: Harcourt Brace Jovanovich.

Evans, E. D., & Warren-Sohlberg, L. A. (1988). A pattern of adolescent abusive behavior towards parents. *Journal of Adolescent Research, 3*(2), 201-216.

Fagan, J. A., Stewart, D. K., & Stewart, K. W. (1983). Situational correlates of domestic and extra-domestic violence. In D. Finkelhor, R. Gelles, G. Hotaling, & M. Straus (Eds.), *The dark side of families: Current family violence research* (pp. 49-67). Beverly Hills, CA: Sage.

Federal Bureau of Investigation. (1985). *Crime in the United States.* Washington, DC: Department of Justice.

Fergusson, D. M., Fleming, J., & O'Neil, D. (1972). *Child abuse in New Zealand.* Wellington, New Zealand: Department of Social Work, Research Division.

Ferreira, A. (1963). Family myth and homeostasis. *Archives of General Psychiatry, 9*(5), 451-463.

Field, M., & Field, H. (1973). Marital violence and the criminal process: Neither justice nor peace. *Social Service Review, 47*(2), 221-240.

Finkelhor, D. (1983). Common features of family abuse. In D. Finkelhor, R. Gelles, G. Hotaling, & M. Straus (Eds.), *The dark side of families: Current family violence research.* (pp. 17-28). Beverly Hills, CA: Sage.

Finkelhor, D., & Yllö, K. (1982). Forced sex in marriage: A preliminary report. *Crime and Delinquency, 28*, 459-478.

Finkelhor, D., & Yllö, K. (1985). *License to rape: Sexual abuse of wives.* New York: Holt, Rinehart & Winston.

Fontana, V. (1973). *Somewhere a child is crying: Maltreatment—causes and prevention.* New York: Macmillan.

144 INTIMATE VIOLENCE IN FAMILIES

Friedrich, W. N., & Boriskin, J. A. (1976). The role of the child in abuse: A review of literature. *American Journal of Orthopsychiatry, 46*(4), 580-590.

Galdston, R. (1965). Observations of children who have been physically abused by their parents. *American Journal of Psychiatry, 122*(4), 440-443.

Galdston, R. (1975). Preventing abuse of little children: The Parent's Center Project for the Study and Prevention of Child Abuse. *American Journal of Orthopsychiatry, 45,* 372-381.

Garbarino, J. (1977). The human ecology of child maltreatment. *Journal of Marriage and the Family, 39*(4), 721-735.

Garbarino, J., & Carlson, B. (1979). *Mistreated youth vs. abused children: Issues for protective services.* Unpublished manuscript.

Garbarino, J., & Gilliam, G. (1980). *Understanding abusive families.* Lexington, MA: Lexington.

Gayford, J. J. (1975). Wife battering: A preliminary survey of 100 cases. *British Medical Journal, 1,* 194-197.

Gelles, R. (1973). Child abuse as psychopathology: A sociological critique and reformulation. *American Journal of Orthopsychiatry, 43,* 611-621.

Gelles, R. (1974). *The violent home.* Beverly Hills, CA: Sage.

Gelles, R. (1975). The social construction of child abuse. *American Journal of Orthopsychiatry, 45,* 363-371.

Gelles, R. (1976). Abused wives: Why do they stay? *Journal of Marriage and the Family, 38,* 659-668.

Gelles, R. (1977). Power, sex, and violence: The case of marital rape. *Family Coordinator, 26,* 339-347.

Gelles, R. (1989). Child abuse and violence in single parent families: Parent absence and economic deprivation. *American Journal of Orthopsychiatry, 59*(4), 492-501.

Gelles, R., & Cornell, C. P. (Eds.). (1983). *International perspectives on family violence.* Lexington, MA: Lexington.

Gelles, R., & Edfeldt, A. (1986). Violence towards children in the United States and Sweden. *Child Abuse and Neglect: The International Journal, 10*(4), 501-510.

Gelles, R., & Hargreaves, E. (1981). Maternal employment and violence towards children. *Journal of Family Issues, 2,* 509-530.

Gelles, R., & Harrop, J. (1989). *The risk of abusive violence among children with non-biological parents.* Paper presented at the annual meetings of the National Council on Family Relations, New Orleans.

Gelles, R., & Harrop, J. (1989, December). Violence, battering, and psychological distress among women. *Journal of Interpersonal Violence, 4,* 400-420.

Gelles, R., & Straus, M. (1979). Determinants of violence in the family: Toward a theoretical integration. In W. R. Burr et al. (Eds.), *Contemporary theories about the family* (Vol. 1). New York: Free Press.

Gelles, R., & Straus, M. (1987). Is violence towards children increasing? A comparison of 1975 and 1985 national survey rates. *Journal of Interpersonal Violence, 2,* 212-222.

Gelles, R., & Straus, M. (1988). *Intimate violence.* New York: Simon & Schuster.

Gil, D. (1970). *Violence against children: Physical child abuse in the United States.* Cambridge, MA: Harvard University Press.

Giles-Sims, J. (1983). *Wife-beating: A systems theory approach.* New York: Guilford.

Giles-Sims, J., & Finkelhor, D. (1984). Child abuse in stepfamilies. *Family Relations, 33,* 407-413.

Gillen, J. (1946). *The Wisconsin prisoner: Studies in crimogenesis.* Madison: University of Wisconsin Press.

Giovannoni, J. M., & Becerra, R. M. (1979). *Defining child abuse.* New York: Free Press.

Gondolf, E. W. (1987). Evaluating progress for men who batter: Problems and prospects. *Journal of Family Violence, 2,* 95-108.

Goode, W. (1971). Force and violence in the family. *Journal of Marriage and the Family, 33,* 624-636.

Guttmacher, M. (1960). *The mind of the murderer.* New York: Farrar, Straus, and Cudahy.

Hampton, R. L., Gelles, R. J., & Harrop, J. W. (1989). Is violence in Black families increasing? A comparison of 1975 and 1985 national survey rates. *Journal of Marriage and the Family , 51*(4), 969-980.

Harbin, H., & Madden, D. (1979). Battered parents: A new syndrome. *American Journal of Psychiatry, 136,* 1288-1291.

Hawalek, M., Senstock, M. C., & Lawrence, R. (1984). *Assessing the probability of abuse of the elderly.* Paper presented at the annual meetings of the Gerontological Society of America, San Antonio, TX.

Henton, J., Cate, R., Koval, J., Lloyd, S., & Christopher, S. (1983). Romance and violence in dating relationships. *Journal of Family Issues, 4,* 467-482.

Herrenkohl, E. C., Herrenkohl, R. C., & Toedler, L. J. (1983). Perspectives on the intergenerational transmission of abuse. In D. Finkelhor, R. Gelles, G. Hotaling, & M. Straus (Eds.), *The dark side of families: Current family violence research* (pp. 305-316). Beverly Hills, CA: Sage.

Hilberman, E. (1980). Overview: "The wife-beater's wife" reconsidered. *American Journal of Psychiatry, 137,* 1336-1346.

Hilberman, E., & Munson, K. (1977). Sixty battered women. *Victimology, 2*(3/4), 460-470.

Homans, G. C. (1967). Fundamental social processes. In N. Smelser (Ed.), *Sociology* (pp. 27-78). New York: John Wiley.

Hornung, C., McCullough, B., & Sugimoto, T. (1981). Status relationships in marriage: Risk factors in spouse abuse. *Journal of Marriage and the Family, 43,* 679-692.

Hotaling, G. T., & Sugarman, D. B. (1986). An analysis of risk markers in husband to wife violence: The current state of knowledge. *Violence and Victims, 1,* 101-124.

Hunter, R., & Kilstrom, N. (1979). Breaking the cycle of abusive families. *American Journal of Psychiatry, 136,* 1320-1322.

Hunter, R., Kilstrom, N., Kraybill, E. N., & Loda, F. (1978). Antecedents of child abuse and neglect in premature infants: A prospective study in a newborn intensive care unit. *Pediatrics, 61,* 629-635.

Jason, J., Carpenter, M., & Tyler, C., Jr. (1983). Underrecording of infant homicide in the United States. *American Journal of Public Health, 73,* 195-197.

Jason, J., Gilliland, J., & Tyler, C., Jr. (1983). Homicide as a cause of pediatric mortality in the United States. *Pediatrics, 72*(2), 191-197.

Jeffrey, M. (1976). Practical ways to change parent-child interaction in families of children at risk. In R. Helfer & C. H. Kempe (Eds.), *Child abuse and neglect: The family and the community* (pp. 209-224). Cambridge, MA: Ballinger.

Johnson, B., & Morse, H. (1968). *The battered child: A study of children with inflicted injuries.* Denver: Denver Department of Welfare.

Johnson, R. (1974). *Aggression in man and animals.* Philadelphia: W. B. Saunders.

Jones, A. (1980). *Women who kill.* New York: Holt, Rinehart & Winston.

Kamerman, S. (1975). Eight countries: Cross-national perspectives on child abuse and neglect. *Children Today, 4*(3), 34-37.

Kaufman, J., & Zigler, E. (1987). Do abused children become abusive parents? *American Journal of Orthopsychiatry, 57*(2), 186-192.

Kantor, G., & Straus, M. (1987). The drunken bum theory of wife beating. *Social Problems, 34*, 213-230.

Kempe, C. H. (1973). A practical approach to the protection of the abused child: Rehabilitating the abusing parent. *Pediatrics, 51*(11), 804-809.

Kempe, C. H., & Helfer, R. (1974). *Helping the battered child and his family.* Philadelphia: J. P. Lippincott.

Kempe, C. H., Silverman, F. N., Steele, B. F., Droegemueller, W., & Silver, H. K. (1962). The battered child syndrome. *Journal of the American Medical Association, 181*, 107-112.

Koch, L., & Koch, J. (1980, January 27). Parent abuse—a new plague. *Washington Post,* pp. PA14-PA15.

Kohn, M. (1977). *Class and conformity: A study of values.* Chicago: University of Chicago Press.

Korbin, J. (Ed.). (1981). *Child abuse and neglect: Cross-cultural perspectives.* Berkeley: University of California Press.

Lane, K. E., & Gwartney-Gibbs, P. A. (1985). Violence in the context of dating and sex. *Journal of Family Issues, 6*(1), 45-59.

Laner, M., Thampson, J., & Graham, R. (1981). *Abuse and aggression in courting couples.* Paper presented at the annual meetings of the Western Social Science Association, San Diego.

Laslett, B. (1973). Family membership, past and present. *Social Problems, 25*(5), 476-490.

Laslett, B. (1978). The family as a public and private institution: A historical perspective. *Journal of Marriage and the Family, 35*, 480-492.

Lau, E. E., & Kosberg, J. I. (1979). Abuse of the elderly by informal care providers. *Aging, 299*, 10-15.

Lauer, B. (1974). Battered child syndrome: Review of 130 patients with controls. *Pediatrics, 54*(1), 67-70.

Legal Research and Services for the Elderly. (1979). *Elder abuse in Massachusetts: A survey of professionals and paraprofessionals.* Unpublished manuscript.

Le Masters, E. (1957). Parenthood as crisis. *Marriage and Family Living, 19*, 352-355.

Leonard, K. E., & Jacob, T. (1988). Alcohol, alcoholism, and family violence. In V. B. Van Hasselt, R. L. Morrison, A. S. Bellack, & M. Hersen (Eds.), *Handbook of family violence* (pp. 383-406). New York: Plenum.

Levinger, G. (1966). Sources of marital dissatisfaction among applicants for divorce. *American Journal of Orthopsychiatry, 26*, 803-897.

Levinson, D. (1981). Physical punishment of children and wifebeating in cross-cultural perspective. *Child Abuse and Neglect, 5*(4), 193-196.

Light, R. J. (1974). Abused and neglected children in America: A study of alternative policies. *Harvard Educational Review, 43*, 556-598.

London, J. (1978). Images of violence against women. *Victimology, 2*(3/4), 510-524.

Lourie, I. (1977). The phenomenon of the abused adolescent: A clinical study. *Victimology, 2*(2), 268-276.

Lourie, I. (1979). Family dynamics and the abuse of adolescents: A case for a developmental phase specific model of child abuse. *Child Abuse and Neglect: The International Journal, 3*, 967-974.

Lyman, S., & Scott, M. (1970). *A sociology of the absurd.* New York: Appleton-Century-Crofts.

MacAndrew, C., & Edgerton, R. B. (1969). *Drunken comportment: A social explanation.* Chicago: Aldine.

Makepeace, J. (1981). Courtship violence among college students. *Family Relations, 30,* 97-102.

Makepeace, J. (1983). Life events-stress and courtship violence. *Family Relations, 32*(1), 101-109.

Margolin, G., Sibner, L. G., & Gleberman, L. (1988). Wife battering. In V. B. Van Hasselt, R. L. Morrison, A. S. Bellack, & M. Hersen (Eds.), *Handbook of family violence* (pp. 89-118). New York: Plenum.

Martin, H. P., Beezley, P., Conway, E. G., & Kempe, C. H. (1974). The development of abused children. In I. Schulman (Ed.), *Advances in pediatrics* (Vol. 21). Chicago: Yearbook Medical.

Maurer, A. (1976). *Physical punishment of children.* Paper presented at the California State Psychological Convention, Anaheim.

McNeeley, R. L., & Robinson-Simpson, G. (1987). The truth about domestic violence: A falsely framed issue. *Social Work, 32*(6), 485-490.

Merton, R. K. (1945). Sociological theory. *American Journal of Sociology, 50,* 462-473.

Mills, C. W. (1940). Situated actions and vocabularies of motive. *American Sociological Review, 5,* 904-913.

Mitchell, L. (1989). Report on fatalities from NCPCA. *Protecting Children, 6*(1), 3-5.

Mulligan, M. (1977). *An investigation of factors associated with violent modes of conflict resolution in the family.* Unpublished master's thesis, University of Rhode Island.

Nagi, R. (1975). Child abuse and neglect programs: A national overview. *Children Today, 4,* 13-17.

National Center on Child Abuse and Neglect. (1988). *Study findings: Study of national incidence and prevalence of child abuse and neglect: 1988.* Washington, DC: U.S. Department of Health and Human Services.

Nelson, B. J. (1984). *Making an issue of child abuse: Political agenda setting for social problems.* Chicago: University of Chicago Press.

Newberger, E. et al. (1977). Pediatric social illness: Toward an etiologic classification. *Pediatrics, 60,* 178-185.

Nye, F. I. (1979). Choice, exchange, and the family. In W. R. Burr et al. (Eds.), *Contemporary theories about the family* (Vol. 2, pp. 1-41). New York: Free Press.

O'Brien, J. (1971). Violence in divorce prone families. *Journal of Marriage and the Family, 33,* 692-698.

O'Leary, K. D. (1988). Physical aggression between spouses: A social learning perspective. In V. B. Van Hasselt, R. L. Morrison, A. S. Bellack, & M. Hersen (Eds.), *Handbook of family violence* (pp. 31-55). New York: Plenum.

Olson, L., & Holmes, W. (1986). Youth at risk: Adolescents and maltreatment. *Children and Youth Services Review, 8,* 13-135.

Owens, D., & Straus, M. A. (1975). Childhood violence and adult approval of violence. *Aggressive Behavior, 1*(2), 193-211.

Pagelow, M. (1981). *Women-battering: Victims and their experiences.* Beverly Hills, CA: Sage.

Pagelow, M. (1989). The incidence and prevalence of criminal abuse of other family members. In L. Ohlin & M. Tonry (Eds.), *Family violence* (pp. 263-313). Chicago: University of Chicago Press.

148   INTIMATE VIOLENCE IN FAMILIES

Parke, R. D., & Collmer, C. W. (1975). Child abuse: An interdisciplinary analysis. In M. Hetherington (Ed.), *Review of child development research* (Vol. 5, pp. 1-102). Chicago: University of Chicago Press.

Parnas, R. (1967). The police response to domestic disturbance. *Wisconsin Law Review, 914*, 914-960.

Peek, C., Fisher, J. L., & Kidwell, J. S. (1985). Teenage violence towards parents: A neglected dimension of family violence. *Journal of Marriage and the Family, 47*(4), 1051-1058.

Pillemer, K. (1985). The dangers of dependency: New findings on domestic violence against the elderly. *Social Problems, 33*, 146-158.

Pillemer, K., & Finkelhor, D. (1988). The prevalence of elder abuse: A random sample survey. *The Gerontologist, 28*(1), 51-57.

Pillemer, K., & Suiter, J. (1988). Elder abuse. In V. B. Van Hasselt, R. L. Morrison, A. S. Bellack, & M. Hersen (Eds.), *Handbook of family violence* (pp. 247-270). New York: Plenum.

Pittman, D., & Handy, W. (1964). Patterns in criminal aggravated assault. *Journal of Criminal Law, Criminology, and Police Science, 55*(4), 462-470.

Pizzey, E. (1974). *Scream quietly or the neighbors will hear.* Harmondsworth: Penguin.

Pleck, E., Pleck, J., Grossman, M., & Bart, P. (1978). The battered data syndrome: A comment on Steinmetz's article. *Victimology, 2*(3/4), 680-683.

Pokorny, A. (1965). Human violence: A comparison of homicide, aggravated assault, suicide, and attempted suicide. *Journal of Criminal Law, Criminology, and Police Science, 56*, 488-497.

Police Foundation. (1977). *Domestic violence and the police: Studies in Detroit and Kansas City.* Washington, DC: National Institute of Justice.

Prescott, S., & Letko, C. (1977). Battered women: A social psychological perspective. In M. Roy (Ed.), *Battered women: A psychosociological study of domestic violence* (pp. 72-96). New York: Van Nostrand Reinhold.

Radbill, S. (1980). A history of child abuse and infanticide. In R. Helfer & C. Kempe (Eds.), *The battered child* (3rd ed., pp. 3-20). Chicago: University of Chicago Press.

Rathbone-McCuan, E. (1980). Elderly victims of family violence and neglect. *Social Casework, 61*, 296-304.

Robin, M. (1982). Historical introduction: Sheltering arms: The roots of child protection. In E. H. Newberger (Ed.), *Child abuse* (pp. 1-41). Boston: Little, Brown.

Roscoe, B., & Bernaske, N. (1985). Courtship violence experienced by abused wives: Similarities in patterns of abuse. *Family Relations, 34*, 419-424.

Rosenbaum, A., & O'Leary, K. D. (1981). Marital violence: Characteristics of abusive couples. *Journal of Consulting and Clinical Psychology, 49* 63-71.

Rosenfeld, A., & Newberger, E. H. (1977). Compassion vs. control: Conceptual and practical pitfalls in the broadened definition of child abuse. *Journal of the American Medical Association, 237*, 2086-2088.

Rossi, A. (1968). Transition to parenthood. *Journal of Marriage and the Family, 30*, 26-39.

Rounsaville, B. J. (1978). Theories of marital violence: Evidence from a study of battered women. *Victimology, 3*(1/2), 11-31.

Roy, M. (1977). *Battered women: A psychosociological study of domestic violence.* New York: Van Nostrand Reinhold.

Russell, D. (1980). *The prevalence and impact of marital rape in San Francisco.* Paper presented at the annual meeting of the American Sociological Association, New York.

Sack, W. H., Mason, R., & Higgins, J. E. (1985). The single-parent family and abusive child punishment. *American Journal of Orthopsychiatry, 55*, 252-259.

Sargent, D. (1962). Children who kill—a family conspiracy. *Social Work, 7*, 35-42.

Saunders, D. G., & Hanusa, D. (1986). Cognitive-behavioral treatment for men who batter: The short-term effects of group therapy. *Journal of Family Violence, 1*(4), 357-372.

Schaie, K. W. (1982). America's elderly in the coming decade. In K. W. Schaie & J. Geiwtiz (Eds.), *Adult development and aging*. Boston: Little, Brown.

Schmitt, B., & Kempe, C. H. (1975). Neglect and abuse of children. In V. Vaughan & R. McKay (Eds.), *Nelson textbook of pediatrics*. Philadelphia: W. B. Saunders.

Schultz, L. G. (1960). The wife assaulter. *Journal of Social Therapy, 6*(2), 103-111.

Sedlak, A. (1988). The use and psychological impact of a battered women's shelter. In G. H. Hotaling, D. Finkelhor, J. T. Kirkpatrick, & M. A. Straus (Eds.), *Coping with family violence: Research and policy perspectives* (pp. 122-128). Newbury Park, CA: Sage.

Senstock, M. C., & Liang, J. (1983). Domestic abuse of the aged: Assessing some dimensions of the problem. *Interdisciplinary Topics in Gerontology, 17*, 58-68.

Shainess, N. (1977). Psychological aspects of wife battering. In M. Roy (Ed.), *Battered women: A psychosociological study of domestic violence* (pp. 111-119). New York: Van Nostrand Reinhold.

Sherman, L., & Berk, R. (1984). The specific deterrent effects of arrest for domestic assault. *American Sociological Review, 49*, 261-272.

Simmel, G. (1950). *The sociology of Georg Simmel* (K. Wolf, Ed.). New York: Free Press.

Smith, E. O., & Byrd, L. (1987). External and internal influences on aggression in captive and group-living monkeys. In R. J. Gelles & J. B. Lancaster (Eds.), *Child abuse and neglect: Biosocial dimensions* (pp. 175-199). Hawthorne, NY: Aldine de Gruyter.

Smith, S. (1965). The adolescent murderer. *Archives of General Psychiatry, 13*, 310-319.

Smith, S. (1975). *The battered child syndrome*. London: Butterworths.

Smith, S., Hansen, R., & Noble, S. (1973). Parents of battered babies: A controlled study. *British Medical Journal, 5*(5889), 388-391.

Smith, S., Honigsberger, L., & Smith, C. (1973). E.E.G. and personality factors in baby batterers. *British Medical Journal, 2*, 20-22.

Snell, J. E., Rosenwald, R. J., & Robey, A. (1964). The wifebeaters's wife: A study of interaction. *Archives of General Psychiatry, 11*, 107-113.

Star, B., Clark, C. G., Goetz, K. M., & O'Malia, L. (1979). Psychological aspects of wife battering. *Social Casework, 60*, 479-487.

Stark, R., & McEvoy, J. (1970). Middle class violence. *Psychology Today, 4*, 52-65.

Starr, R. H., Jr. (1982). A research based approach to the prediction of child abuse. In R. H. Starr, Jr., *Child abuse prediction: Policy implications* (pp. 105-142). Cambridge, MA: Ballinger.

Starr, R. H., Jr. (1988). Physical abuse of children. In V. B. Van Hasselt, R. L. Morrison, A. S. Bellack, & M. Hersen (Eds.), *Handbook of family violence* (pp. 119-155). New York: Plenum.

Starr, R. H., Jr., Dietrich, K. N., Fishoff, J., Ceresnie, S., & Demorest, M. (1984). The contribution of handicapping conditions to child abuse. *Topics in Early Childhood Special Education, 4*, 55-69.

State legislation on domestic violence. (1983). *Response, 6*(5), 1-5.

Steele, B. F. (1978). The child abuser. In I. Kutash et al. (Eds.), *Violence perspectives on murder and aggression* (pp. 285-300). San Francisco: Jossey-Bass.

Steele, B. F., & Pollock, C. (1968). A psychiatric study of parents who abuse infants and small children. In R. Helfer & C. Kempe (Eds.), *The battered child* (pp. 89-134). Chicago: University of Chicago Press.

Steinmetz, S. K. (1971). Occupation and physical punishment: A response to Straus. *Journal of Marriage and the Family, 33*, 664-666.

Steinmetz, S. K. (1977). *The cycle of violence: Assertive, aggressive, and abusive family interaction.* New York: Praeger.

Steinmetz, S. K. (1978a). The battered husband syndrome. *Victimology, 2*(3/4), 499-509.

Steinmetz, S. K. (1978b). Violence between family members. *Marriage and Family Review, 1*(3), 1-16.

Steinmetz, S. K. (1978c). Battered parents. *Society, 15*(5), 54-55.

Steinmetz, S. K. (1982). A cross-cultural comparison of sibling violence. *International Journal of Family Psychiatry, 2*(3/4), 337-351.

Steinmetz, S. K. (1987). Family violence: Past, present, and future. In M. B. Sussman & S. K. Steinmetz (Eds.), *Handbook of marriage and the family* (pp. 725-765). New York: Plenum.

Steinmetz, S. K., & Straus, M. (1974). *Violence in the family.* New York: Harper & Row.

Straus, M. (1971). Some social antecedents of physical punishment: A linkage theory interpretation. *Journal of Marriage and the Family, 33*, 658-663.

Straus, M. (1980). A sociological perspective on the causes of family violence. In M. R. Green (Ed.), *Violence and the family* (pp. 7-31). Boulder, CO: Westview.

Straus, M., & Gelles, R. J. (1986). Societal change and family violence from 1975 to 1985 as revealed by two national surveys. *Journal of Marriage and the Family, 48*, 465-479.

Straus, M., & Gelles, R. J. (1988). Violence in American families: How much is there and why does it occur? In E. W. Nunnally, C. Chilman, & F. M. Cox (Eds.), *Troubled relationships* (pp. 141-162). Newbury Park, CA: Sage.

Straus, M., Gelles, R. J., & Steinmetz, S. K. (1976). *Violence in the family: An assessment of knowledge and research needs.* Paper presented at the American Association for the Advancement of Science, Boston.

Straus, M., Gelles, R. J., & Steinmetz, S. K. (1980). *Behind closed doors: Violence in the American family.* Garden City, NY: Anchor.

Straus, M., & Hotaling, G. (1979). *The social causes of husband-wife violence.* Minneapolis: University of Minnesota Press.

Strube, M. J., & Barbour, L. S. (1983). The decision to leave an abusive relationship: Economic dependence and psychological commitment. *Journal of Marriage and the Family, 45*, 785-793.

Sugarman, D., & Hotaling, G. (1989). Dating violence: Prevalence, context, and risk markers. In M. A. Pirog-Good & J. E. Stets (Eds.), *Violence in dating relationships: Emerging issues* (pp. 3-32). New York: Praeger.

Toby, J. (1986). Violence and the masculine ideal: Some qualitative data. *Annals of the American Academy of Political and Social Science, 364*, 20-27.

Tooley, K. (1977). The young child as victim of sibling attack. *Social Casework, 58*(1), 25-28.

Trainor, C. (1984). *A description of officially reported adolescent maltreatment and its implications for policy and practice.* Denver: American Humane Association.

Truninger, E. (1971). Marital violence: The legal solutions. *Hastings Law Review, 23*, 259-276.

Turbett, J. P., & O'Toole, R. (1980). *Physician's recognition of child abuse.* Paper presented at the annual meeting of the American Sociological Association, New York.

U.S. Bureau of the Census. (1978). *Statistical Abstracts of the United States.* Washington, DC: U.S. Department of Commerce.

U.S. Congress, House Select Committee on Aging, Subcommittee on Human Services. (1980). *Domestic abuse of the elderly.* Washington, DC: Government Printing Office.

U.S. Department of Justice. (1980). *Intimate violence: A study of violence among friends and relatives.* Washington, DC: Government Printing Office.

U.S. Department of Justice. (1981). *Uniform Crime Reports, 1980.* Washington, DC: Government Printing Office.

U.S. Department of Justice. (1984a, September). *Attorney General's Task Force on Family Violence: Final report.* Washington, DC: Government Printing Office.

U.S. Department of Justice. (1984b). *Family violence.* Washington, DC: Bureau of Justice Statistics.

U.S. Senate. (1973). Hearing before the Subcommittee on Children and Youth of the Committee on Labor and Public Welfare. U.S. Senate, 93rd Congress, first session, on S.1191 Child Abuse Prevention Act. Washington, DC: Government Printing Office.

Vesterdal, J. (1977). Handling of child abuse in Denmark. *Child Abuse and Neglect, 1*(1), 193-198.

Walker, L. (1979). *The battered woman.* New York: Harper & Row.

Warren, C. (1978). *Battered parents: Adolescent violence and the family.* Paper presented at the Pacific Sociological Association.

Wasserman, S. (1967). The abused parent of the abused child. *Children, 14,* 175-179.

Wauchope, B., & Straus, M. (1990). Age, gender and class differences in physical punishment and physical abuse of American children. In M. Straus & R. J. Gelles (Eds.), *Physical violence in American families: Risk factors and adaptations in 8,145 families* (pp. 133-148). New Brunswick, NJ: Transaction.

Weitzman, J., & Dreen, K. (1982). Wife-beating: A view of the marital dyad. *Social Casework, 63*(5), 259-265.

Wertham, F. (1972). Battered children and baffled parents. *Bulletin of the New York Academy of Medicine, 48,* 888-898.

Widom, C. S. (1989, April 14). The cycle of violence. *Science, 244,* 160-166.

Wilson, M., & Daly, M. (1987). Risk of maltreatment of children living with stepparents. In R. J. Gelles & J. B. Lancaster (Eds.), *Child abuse and neglect: Biosocial dimensions* (pp. 215-232). Hawthorne, NY: Aldine de Gruyter.

Wilson, M., Daly, M., & Weghorst, S. J. (1980). Household composition and the risk of child abuse and neglect. *Journal of Biosocial Science, 12,* 333-340.

Wolf, R., Strugnell, C., & Godkin, M. (1982). *Preliminary findings from three model projects on elderly abuse.* Worcester: University of Massachusetts Medical Center, University Center on Aging.

Wolfgang, M. (1958). *Patterns in criminal homicide.* New York: John Wiley.

Woolley, P., & Evans, W. (1955). Significance of skeletal lesions resembling those of traumatic origin. *Journal of the American Medical Association, 158,* 539-543.

Wright, L. (1971). The "sick but slick" syndrome as a personality component for parents of battered children. *Journal of Clinical Psychology, 32*(1), 41-45.

Young, L. (1964). *Wednesday's child: A study of child neglect and abuse.* New York: McGraw-Hill.

Zalba, S. (1971). Battered children. *Transaction, 8,* 58-61.

Author Index

Adelson, L., 87, 90
Agnew, R., 78, 98, 99
Alfaro, J., 62
American Association for Protecting Children, 47, 51, 53
American Humane Association, 47, 57
Aria, I., 65
Aries, P., 32

Ball, M., 73
Becerra, R., 22
Bender, L., 87
Berk, R., 82
Berk, S., 131, 132
Bernaske, N., 66
Blau, P., 116
Block, M., 103
Blumberg, M., 44
Boriskin, J., 54
Boudouris, J., 67
Bowker, L., 81
Brekke, J., 74
Bronfenbrenner, U., 44
Brownmiller, S., 17
Burgdorf, K., 57
Button, A., 62
Byrd, L., 19

Caffey, J., 33
Carlson, B., 92
Carpenter, M., 50
Carr, A., 62
Cate, R., 66
Ceresine, S., 65
Coleman, D., 19, 74
Collmer, C., 54
Cornell, C., 62, 90, 98
Curtis, L., 67

D'Agostino, S., 40
Daly, M., 56

Davidson, T., 28
DeFrancis, V., 45
De Mause, L., 27
Department of Justice, 133
Demorest, J., 55
Dietrich, K., 55
Dobash, R., 27, 28, 31, 115, 132
Dobash, R. E., 26, 28, 31, 115, 132
Dreen, K., 73
Dunford, F., 132
Dutton, D., 137

Edfeldt, A., 30
Edgerton, R., 18
Egeland, B., 55, 60
Elliot, D., 131
Elmer, E., 54, 59
Erlanger, H., 44
Etzioni, A., 23
Evans, E., 99
Evans, W., 33

Fagan, J., 74, 75
Fergusson, D., 54
Ferreira, A., 97
Field, H., 132
Field, M., 132
Finkelhor, D., 72, 77
Fishoff, J., 55
Fontana, V., 55
Freidrich, W., 54

Garbarino, J., 58, 114, 115
Gayford, J., 74, 75
Gelles, R., 12, 18, 39, 44, 48, 49, 50, 51, 52, 54, 56, 57, 58, 74, 75, 76, 77, 79, 80, 82, 86, 88, 89, 90, 92, 94, 98, 107, 108, 109, 118, 129
Gil, D., 13, 45, 54, 57, 58, 91, 93, 94
Giles-Sims, J., 56, 136
Gillen, J., 18

Gilliam, G., 58
Gilliland, J., 50
Giovannoni, J., 22
Gleberman, L., 73
Godkin, M., 103
Gondolf, E., 137
Goode, W., 95, 96, 113
Guttmacher, M., 18
Gwartney-Gibbs, P., 65

Hampton, R., 51, 70
Handy, W., 23, 67
Hanusa, D., 137
Harbin, H., 96, 97, 98, 99
Hargreaves, E., 58, 118
Harrop, J., 51, 70, 74
Hawalek, M., 103
Helfer, R., 129
Henton, J., 66
Herrenkohl, E., 60
Herrenkohl, R., 60
Higgins, J., 56
Hilberman, E., 77
Holmes, W., 92
Hornung, C., 76
Hotaling, G., 109
Huguley, S., 98, 99
Huizinga, D., 143
Hunter, R., 59

Jacob, T., 55
Jacobvitz, D., 59, 60
Jason, J., 50
Jeffrey, M., 129
Johnson, B., 58
Johnson, C., 54
Johnson, R., 19

Kantor, G., 19, 74
Kamerman, S., 28
Kempe, C., 20, 33, 62, 129
Kilstrom, N., 59
Koch, J., 100
Koch, L., 100
Kohn, M., 57
Korbin, J., 31
Kosberg, J. 101
Kraybill, E., 59

Lane, K., 65
Laslett, B., 118
Lau, E., 101
Lauer, B., 57
Lawrence, R., 103
Legal Research and Services for the Elderly, 101, 103
Leonard, K., 55
Letko, C., 75
Levinger, G., 15, 67
Levinson, D., 29
Liang, J., 103, 104
Light, R., 45
Loda, F., 59
London, J., 23
Loseke, D., 131, 132
Lourie, I., 92, 95
Lyman, S., 119

MacAndrew, C., 18
Madden, D., 96, 97, 98, 99
Makepiece, J., 66
Margolin, G., 73
Martin, M., 55
Mason, R., 56
McEvoy, J., 21, 36, 44, 85
McNeeley, R., 82
Merton, R., 116
Mills, C. W., 119
Mitchel, L., 50
Morse, H., 58
Mullingon, M., 45, 93, 94, 97
Munson, K., 77

Nagi, S., 45
National Center on Child Abuse and Neglect, 20, 46
Nelson, B., 33
Newberger, E., 15, 53, 54, 111, 126, 127
Newton, P., 137
Nye, F., 117, 120

O'Brien, J., 67, 76
O'Leary, K., 65, 76
Olsen, L., 92
O'Toole, R., 54
Owens, D., 41

Pagelow, M., 79, 102
Papatola, K., 60
Parke, R., 54
Parnas, R., 125
Peek, C., 98
Pillemer, K., 102, 104
Pittman, D., 23, 67
Pizzey, E., 37
Pokorny, A, 23
Police Foundation, 131
Pollock, C., 54
Prescott, S., 75

Radbill, S., 26, 32
Rathbone-McCuan, E., 103
Robey, A., 18
Robin, M., 27, 32
Robinson-Simpson, G., 82
Roscoe, B., 66
Rosenfeld, A., 126, 127
Rosenwald, R., 18
Rousaville, B., 75, 76
Roy, M., 76
Russell, D., 72

Sack, W., 56
Samios, M., 65
Sargent, D., 86, 87
Saunders, D., 74, 137
Schaie, K., 103
Schmitt, B., 62
Scott, M., 119
Sedlak, A., 136
Senstock, M., 103, 104
Shainess, N., 73
Sherman, L., 132
Sibner, L., 72
Simmel, G., 110
Sinnott, J., 103
Smith, E. O., 19
Smith, S., 55, 58, 62, 87
Snell, J., 18, 73
Sroufe, A., 59, 60
Star, B., 73
Stark, R., 21, 36, 44, 85
Starr, R., 54, 55, 56, 62
Steele, B., 54, 112

Steinmetz, S., 12, 14, 39, 44, 48, 49, 50, 51, 54, 56, 67, 58, 59, 74, 76, 77, 82, 85, 86, 87, 88, 89, 91, 92, 94, 98, 103, 107, 108, 129
Straus, M., 12, 14, 39, 41, 48, 49, 50, 51, 52, 54, 56, 57, 58, 74, 75, 77, 81, 82, 86, 88, 89, 92, 94, 98, 107, 108, 109, 112, 129
Strugnell, C., 103
Sugarman, D., 65
Suiter, J., 103, 104

Toby, J., 119
Toedler, L., 60
Tooley, K., 90
Trainor, C., 92
Truninger, E., 79
Turbett, J., 54
Tyler, C., 50

U.S. Bureau of the Census, 100
U.S. Congress, 102
U.S. Department of Justice, 68

Vaughan, B., 55
Vesterdal, J., 30

Walker, L., 73, 78
Walters, J., 55
Warren, C., 96
Warren-Sohlberg, L., 99
Wasserman, S., 59
Wauchope, B., 49, 57, 94
Weghorst, S., 56
Weisfield, G., 62
Weitzman, J., 73
Wertham, F., 55
Widom, C. S., 62
Wilson, M., 56
Wolf, R., 103
Wolfgang, M., 18, 23
Woolley, P., 33
Wright, L., 55

Yllö, K., 72
Young, L., 55

Subject Index

Abortion, 26, 30
Abusive violence, 23-24, 49-50
Abuser
  child abuse, 50-51, 54-57, 118
  power issues, 72-73, 76
  social class of, 57-58, 75
  spouse abuser, 17, 72-74, 118
  treatment, 137
  working mothers, 58
Adolescent violence
  characteristics of abused, 93-94
  frequency of, 92-93
  normative attitudes toward, 90-91
  parental expectations, 91
  prevention, 126
  size and strength of abuse, 91-92
Age
  of abuser, 57, 75, 98, 103
  of victim, 49, 54-55, 89-90, 93-94, 103, 120
Alcohol, 18-19, 56, 74, 111, 119
American Humane Association, 47
Amphetamines, 19
Appropriate victims of family violence, 27-28, 65
Assault, 23

"Battered Child Syndrome," 20
Biblical accounts
  of child abuse, 25
  of spouse abuse, 27-28
Blackstone, 28
Blaming the victim, 17, 66-67, 85, 90-91, 96-97, 101
Brother to Brother, 137

Canada, rates of family violence, 28
Child abuse, 13, 26-27, 42, 45-52
  and value of children, 30-31
  changing rates, 50-52

child factors as contributing to, 114-115
cross-cultural studies of, 28-29
definition of, 20-24, 47
diagnosis of, 16-17, 33, 42
frequency of, 43, 45
historical legacy of, 26-28
legislation, 33-34, 36
profile of violent home, 106-108
reporting programs, 51-52, 123-124
treatment programs for, 35, 128-130
Child Abuse Prevention Act, 35
Child factors as associated with child abuse, 54-55, 114-115, 119
Child welfare services, 128-129
Children's Bureau, 35
China and family violence, 30, 31
Compassion model, 122-123, 126-128
Comprehensive Child Development Act, 36
Conflict tactics scale, 48, 68
Consequences of child abuse, 61-63
Contemporary attitudes of family violence, 38-40
Contraceptives, 30
Control model, 127-128
Cotton Mather, 32
Courts' involvement in domestic violence, 135
Courtship violence
  frequency, 65-66
  romantic illusions, 66
Crack abuse, 19
Criminal assault, 67
Criminal justice system, 32, 43, 67-68, 123-125, 135-136
Criminalization of spouse abuse, 124-126
Cross-cultural studies of violence
  alcohol as related to, 18-19
  attitudes toward women and children, 30-31

causes of, 28-31
definitions of abuses, 28-29
frequency of, 29
Culpability as related to wife abuse, 17,
    20, 66-67
Cultural attitudes toward family vio-
    lence, 22, 39-30, 39-41, 112-114, 120,
    139
"Cycle of Violence" theory, 16-17, 40-41,
    58-60, 75-76, 99, 104-105, 122-123,
    139
    in China, 30, 31

Data collection techniques, 47, 69-70
    for adolescent violence, 94
    for sibling violence, 86-87
    in clinical research, 53-54
    in survey research, 49, 53-54
    use of official reports, 53
Day care institutions, 30
Delinquency as a result of child abuse,
    61-63
Demographic factors
    adolescent abuse, 93-95
    child abuse, 56-57
    elder abuse, 100, 102
    parent abuse, 98-99
    sibling violence, 88-90
    spouse abuse, 74-75
Developed nations, rates of violence, 29-
    31
Divorce, 15, 67-68, 78-79, 118
Doctors' role, 15-16, 20-21, 33, 53-54, 64
Domestic disturbance, 13, 67
Drugs, 18-19, 56, 111

Ecological perspective, 114-115
Economic factors
    of child abuse, 57-58
    of spouse abuse, 75
Education for parenting, 129
Elder abuse
    definition of, 102-103
    factors relating to, 103-104
    frequency of, 102
    social awareness of, 101-102
    societal attitudes toward, 101
    treatment of, 126, 137

Emerge, 137
Emotional abuse, 147
Exchange/social control theory, 115-121

Fairy tales, 40
Family life
    as a refuge, 11, 13-14
    extended family, 119-120
    organization of, 108-110, 122
    privacy of, 40
Family violence
    approval of, 25-26
    as portrayed by media, 14, 23, 26, 40
    causal explanations of, 15-16, 18, 40-41
    definition of, 20-24
    frequency of, 13, 20, 25, 29
    myths about, 12-20
Feminism, 23
Figgie Report, 38
First National Family Violence Survey, 57,
    71
Force, 21-22, 114
France, rate of family violence, 29-30

Genovese, Kitty, 39-40
Germany, rate of family violence, 29-30
Great Britain, occurrences of family vio-
    lence, 29-30

Harris, Louis, 25
Historical legacy of violence, 26-28
Home care of the elderly, 101, 103
Homicide, 23
    child, 50
    siblings, 90
    spousal, 67
Husband abuse, 81-82

Illegitimacy, 27
Individual factors associated with spouse
    abuse, 72-74
Inequality as related to family violence,
    36-37, 115, 117-119, 139
Infanticide, 26-27
Injury, 20-24, 25, 43-44, 47-49, 61-62, 68-69
Institutionalization of the elderly, 101, 138
Intention of abusive behavior, 21-24, 42,
    44, 102

Intervention, lack of, 25, 39-40
Isolation
    child abuse, 58, 114
    elder abuse, 100
    family violence, 139
    spouse abuse, 77-78

Jolly K., 36

Learned helplessness, 78
Love, 18-19, 66
LSD, 19

Mandatory arrest, 132-135
Marital rape, 72
Masochistic women, 73, 78
Media, treatment of family violence, 14,
    23, 26, 40
Mental illness as a cause of abusive behav-
    ior, 13-14, 55, 111, 122
Mesopotamia, 31
Milkulski, B., 37
Minneapolis Police Experiment, 131
Models that explain family violence, 111-
    115
Mondale, W., 35
Murder, 62, 96
Myths that hinder recognition of family
    violence, 12-20

National Center on Child Abuse and
    Neglect, 20, 21, 46
National Domestic Violence Prevention
    and Treatment Act, 37
National Enquirer, 26
National Institute of Justice, 133
National Organization for Women, 37
National Study of Child Neglect and
    Abuse Reporting, 46-47
Nixon, R., 36
"Normal" violence, 21-23, 25-26, 38-40,
    43-44, 86
Normative attitudes toward violence,
    112, 114
    and adolescent violence, 90-92
    and elder abuse, 100-102
    and parent abuse, 95-97
    and sibling violence, 85-87

Nussbaum, Hedda, 14-15, 17

Omaha, 134
Organization of family life as contributing
    to violence, 108-110

Parent abuse
    and the cycle of violence, 99
    factors related to, 98-99
    frequency of, 97-98
    normative attitudes toward, 96-97
    reporting of, 96
    role of denial in, 99
    treatment of, 126, 137
Parent factors associated with child
    abuse, 55-56
Parents Anonymous, 36, 129
Patriarchy and wife abuse, 115
Physical punishment, 43-44, 110
Police, 13, 21, 67, 78, 117-118, 125, 130-132
Police Foundation, 133
Pornography, 23
Power, 73, 76, 118
Prevention
    of child abuse, 123-124
    of family violence, 121, 138-139
    of hidden forms of violence, 126-127
Privacy, 39-40, 110, 117-119, 122-123
Profile of violent homes
    child abuse, 106-108
    spouse abuse, 108-110
Prosecution, 135
Psychiatric model of family violence, 111-
    112
Psychological portraits of abused women,
    72-74

Race
    of abuser, 53, 57
    of victim, 53, 57
"Read Man" image, 118-119
Relationship factors associated with
    spouse abuse, 76-77
Reporting laws, 13, 33-34, 123-124, 126,
    137
Resource theory, 113-114
Resources and decision to stay or leave
    abusive situation, 78-81

"Revenge is sweet," 119
Rewards and punishment, 116-117
Risk, 16-17, 54-55, 108-109, 114-115, 119-121
Rule of thumb, 28

Scandinavian countries, rates of family violence, 30
Second National Family Violence Survey, 48, 69, 81, 135
Self-fulfilling prophecy, 125
Sex
    of abuser, 55, 98-99, 102
    of victim, 54, 88-89, 93-94, 98, 102
Sexual abuse, 47
Shelters for battered women, 37, 79, 126, 130-131, 135-137
Sibling rivalry, 85-86
Sibling violence, 11, 25
    as a learned response, 90
    factors associated with, 88-90
    frequency of, 87-88
    normative attitudes toward, 85-87
    treatment of, 138
Social awareness
    of adolescent abuse, 90
    of elder abuse, 100-104
    of parent abuse, 95-96
    of sibling violence, 87
Social class and association
    with child abuse, 52, 57
    with family violence, 14-15
    with incorrect labeling of abusers, 15-16, 53
    with spouse abuse, 75
Social control, 117-120, 122-123
Social learning theory, 12, 40-41, 90, 99, 104, 113

Social-psychological model of child abuse, 60-61
Social workers, 21, 42-43, 64-65, 78--79
Spanking, 21, 22, 43-44, 116, 120
"Spare the rod . . .," 22
Spouse abuse
    and decision to stay or leave, 17, 78-81
    cross-cultural studies of, 27-28, 36-37
    definition of, 20
    factors related to, 13, 17
    frequency of, 27-28, 36-37, 66-67, 69
    legislation regarding, 37, 124-125
    profile of violent home, 107-108
    shelters for victims of, 37, 126, 131, 135-136
    treatment of, 130-137
    victims of, 27-28, 64-65, 72-78
Status incompatibility, 76
Status inconsistency, 766
Steinberg, Joel, 14-15, 17
Steinberg, Lisa, 14-15, 17
Stress as related to
    adolescent abuse, 94
    child abuse, 58
    elder abuse, 104
    family violence, 110, 139
    spouse abuse, 78
    structure of family, 112-113

Thurman, Tracy, 133
Torrington, Connecticut, 133
Treatment, 121, 128-138

U.S. Commission on the Causes and Prevention of Violence, 38
U.S. Attorney General's Task Force on Family Violence, 37

Wilson, Mary Ellen, 32-33, 34

About the Authors

Richard J. Gelles is Dean of the College of Arts and Sciences and Professor of Sociology and Anthropology at the University of Rhode Island. He directs the Family Violence Research Program at the University of Rhode Island and is the author or coauthor of 11 books and more than 60 articles and chapters on family violence. His most recent books are *Intimate Violence* (1988, Simon & Schuster) and *Physical Violence in American Families: Risk Factors and Adaptations in 8,145 Families* (1990, Transaction Books). In addition, he is coauthor of two sociology textbooks and author of numerous articles on family studies, media studies, and research methodology.

Claire Pedrick Cornell was formerly Special Instructor of Sociology and Anthropology at the University of Rhode Island and Research Analyst with the Family Violence Research Program at the University of Rhode Island. Her research interests include child abuse, spouse abuse, adolescent violence, and abuse of the elderly. She is coeditor of *International Perspectives on Family Violence* (1983). She currently resides in Canada and is on a hiatus while caring for her young son.

NOTES